# The Theory of Interest
## Robertson versus Keynes
## and
## The Long-Period Problem of
## Saving and Debt

# Third Edition

# The Theory of Interest
### Robertson versus Keynes
### and
### The Long-Period Problem of
### Saving and Debt

# Third Edition

ISBN: 978-1-712583-79-1

www.rwEconomics.com is an imprint of
DMC Software, Inc.

It is here enough to repeat that Free Trade can nowise guarantee the maintenance of industry, or of an industrial population upon any particular country, and there is no consideration, theoretic or practical, to prevent British capital from transferring itself to China, provided it can find there a cheaper or more efficient supply of labour, or even to prevent Chinese capital with Chinese labour from ousting British produce in neutral markets of the world. What applies to Great Britain applies equally to the other industrial nations which have driven their economic suckers into China. It is at least conceivable that China might so turn the tables upon the Western industrial nations, and, either by adopting their capital and organisers or, as is more probable, by substituting her own, might flood their markets with her cheaper manufactures, and refusing their imports in exchange might take her payment in liens upon their capital, reversing the earlier process of investment until she gradually obtained financial control over her quondam patrons and civilisers. This is no idle speculation. If China in very truth possesses those industrial and business capacities with which she is commonly accredited, and the Western Powers are able to have their will in developing her upon Western lines, it seems extremely likely that this reaction will result.

John Atkinson Hobson
*Imperialism, A Study*
1902.

In memory of my parents
George Philip and Marion White Blackford

and grandparents
George and Juanita Cuvrell Blackford
Henry Jacob and Mary Baumgartner White

# Dedication

To the very talented and highly dedicated mentors I have had the privilege of being influenced by in my tender years: Ms. Shegus, Ms. Lockner, Ms. Fortiner, Neil Cason, Charles Shinn, Joseph T. Davis, William H. Whitemore, Chris and Robert Anderlik, Frank Jackson, William M. Armstrong, Florence A. Kirk, Louis R. Miner, Louis Toller, Alfred C. Raphelson, Elston W. Van Steenburgh, Paul G. Bradley, Virgil M. Bett, W. H. Locke Anderson, Daniel B. Suits, Kenneth E. Boulding, Saul H. Hymans, Cliff L. Lloyd, James Crotty, Ray Boddy, Winston Chang, Nagesh S. Revankar, and Mitchell Harwitz.

Each of these individuals has had a profoundly positive influence on my life, and I will be indebted to each forever. This is especially so with regard to Ms. Fortiner, Joseph T. Davis, Charles Shinn, William H. Whitemore, Robert and Chris Anderlik, Alfred C. Raphelson, Elston W. Van Steenburgh, Virgil M. Bett, Daniel B. Suits, Kenneth E. Boulding, W. H. Locke Anderson, Ray Boddy, Cliff Lloyd, James Crotty, Nagesh S. Revankar, and Mitchell Harwitz.

Then there are the kids: To Heidi, Steve, Robin, Terry, Jamie, Cherilyn, Brad, Terri, Mark, Leigh, Bobby, Sandy, Cindy, Tony, Chelsea, Jeremy, Jason, Stephanie, Shannon, Joe, Stevie, Charlene, Elizabeth, Nathan, Jessica, Donnie, David, Claire, Ryan, Andrea, Ashley, Tauri, Brandon, Brian, Shawna, Aaron, Maria, Anna, Caley, Sam, Emma, Alex, Aidan, Lucas, Joey, Sophia, Maxwell, Lily, Brily, Jason Jr., and Carter. What does it all mean without them? It is for them that I have written this manuscript in the hope it will contribute toward a better understanding of the world in which we live and toward a better future for all of our children.

The changes in the text of this edition are primarily editorial, designed to strengthen the argument. The formal modes specified in **Appendix A: Keynes' Theory of Interest** and **Appendix B: the Structure of Keynes' Model** of earlier editions are not included in this edition. They have been substantially revised and are included in the forthcoming ***Essays on Political Economy Volume III: Keynes***.

George H. Blackford
November 4, 2019

## Also by George H. Blackford

### *Where Did All The Money Go?*
**How Lower Taxes, Less Government, and Deregulation Redistribute Income and Create Economic Instability**

### *Essays on Political Economy*
*Volume I: Reality*
*Volume II: Ideology*
*Volume III: Keynes*

### *Understanding the Federal Budget (2013)*
**What the taxes and expenditures of the federal government actually look like in the real world**

# Preface to First Edition

In the Preface to *The General Theory of Employment, Interest, and Money,* John Maynard Keynes wrote:

> The composition of this book has been for the author a long struggle of escape, and so must the reading of it be for most readers if the author's assault upon them is to be successful,—a struggle of escape from habitual modes of thought and expression. The ideas which are here expressed so laboriously are extremely simple and should be obvious. The difficulty lies, not in the new ideas, but in escaping from the old ones, which ramify, for those brought up as most of us have been, into every corner of our minds. (1936, p. viii)

It is argued below that the failure of policy makers to escape the old and accept the new led to the adoption of economic policies over the past forty-five years that culminated in the Crash of 2008 and the economic stagnation that followed. It is further argued that this failure arose from an inability to appreciate the role of Marshall in the development of Keynes' thought. I find Keynes' simple ideas to be easily understood from the perspective of Marshall and beyond the ken of the Walrasian paradigm of neoclassical economics that underlies the worldview of policy makers.

While the primary purpose of this monograph is to provide a definitive explanation of the way in which the rate of interest is determined and to explain the connection between the central thesis of The General Theory and the economic problems we face today, the manuscript is written in such a way as to explain Keynes' general theory from the perspective of Marshall. As such, it is a primer on The General Theory of Employment, Interest, and Money, directed toward economics students in the hope that it will facilitate their ability to go beyond the Walrasian perspective of Neoclassical economics to gain a deeper understanding of Keynes and of the way in which the economic system actually works in the real world.

George H. Blackford
December 15, 20

# Table of Contents

# Prologue[*]

In November of 1936, Dennis H. Robertson proclaimed: "it is not as a refutation of a common-sense account of events in terms of supply and demand for loanable funds, but as an alternative version of it, that Mr. Keynes' account as finally developed must be regarded." (p.183) The following February, Keynes asked Robertson to provide "at least one reference as to where this common-sense account is to be found." (p. 210) Thus began the controversy that evolved into what became known as the liquidity-preference/loanable-funds (LP/LF) debate. This debate continued long after Keynes' death in 1946 when the torch was passed from Keynes to the Keynesians.

With the Keynesians in charge, the debate took a decidedly Walrasian turn. While some Keynesians may have continued to defend Keynes' argument from *A Treatise on Money* to the effect that the rate of interest cannot change in response to a change in saving or investment in the absence of a change in income, the vast majority fully embraced John R. Hicks' 1936 argument to the effect that it makes no difference which theory one accepts since the static equilibrium properties of the two theories are the same. The

[*] I would like to thank Gillian G. Garcia for her insightful and critical comments that have helped immensely to clarify the issues for me. I would also like to thank David Glasner for his knowledgeable, patient, and open-minded responses to my comments on his blog, responses that motivated me to resurrect the research I had done in the nineteen seventies and eighties and bring it up to date. And then there is Kathryn J. Ross and Dolores M. Coulter to whom I am deeply indebted for their relentless efforts to dismantle my run-on sentences and force me to abide by the rules of grammar and spelling as best they could.

Keynesians embraced this argument in spite of the fact that Keynes had rejected it in June of 1937.

In response to the Keynesians, Robertson and his fellow anti-Keynesians continued to insist that Keynes was wrong in his rejection of the idea that the rate of interest is determined by saving and investment through the supply and demand for loanable funds irrespective of whether the equilibrium properties of the two theories are the same. The position of the anti-Keynesians was best summarized by Harry Johnson in 1961:

> The liquidity preference-loanable funds debate turns on the question of whether the rate of interest is better regarded as equilibrating the flow of funds onto and off the market for securities or as equilibrating the demand for and supply of the stock of cash. The answer... seems to be that...it makes no difference...provided... one is concerned only with the determination of the equilibrium level of the rate of interest.... The two theories become different, however, when applied to dynamic analysis of disequilibrium situations.... In a dynamic context, the loanable-funds theory definitely makes more economic sense; and the sustained resistance of Keynesians to admitting it, evident most notably in the prolonged defense...of the proposition that an increase in the propensity to save lowers the interest rate only by reducing the level of income, is a credit to their ingenuity rather than their scientific spirit. (1961, pp. 6-7)

And so it went until Robertson died in 1963, a point in time at which the Keynesians so dominated the discipline of economics that there seemed to be no need for them to continue to respond to the anti-Keynesians on this issue, and the controversy just petered out.

Since it made no difference to the Keynesians which theory was assumed, the Keynesians walked away from the debate confident they were victorious as they concentrated on the equilibrium properties of their models. And since the anti-Keynesians were no longer rebuffed by the Keynesians, the anti-Keynesians walked away equally confident of the victorious nature of their performance. Thus, the debate ended with both sides declaring victory. As a result, the issues of the Robertson/Keynes controversy have never been resolved, for while it is generally agreed that the two theories have identical static equilibrium properties, *there exists no consensus as to the nature of their dynamic properties.*[1]

The failure to achieve a consensus in this regard has had the gravest of consequences for it left the discipline of economics with two theories of interest, each of which seems plausible and neither of which is fully understood. The result has been a persistent ambiguity with regard to numerous theoretical and practical problems relating to the way in which *saving* affects the economic system. The reason is, Keynes argued throughout *The General Theory* that saving is a nemesis that plagues the economic system by inhibiting economic growth and employment. It was this argument that Robertson challenged in his controversy with Keynes. Thus, even though the primary focus

---

[1] With regard to this equivalence and lack of consensus on the dynamic properties of the two theories see Ackley (1957), Asimakopulos, Brunner, Davidson, Fellner and Somers, Fleisher and Kopecky, Modigliani, Palley, Horwich, Johnson, Keynes, Klein, Kohn, Lerner, Lloyd, Patinkin, Robertson, Robinson, Rose, Stiglitz (1999), Terzi, Tsiang, and Wray. For surveys of the early literature see Haberler, Shackle, and Johnson (1962). For an analysis of the later literature see Bibow (2009).

of the LP/LF debate was on the determination of the rate of interest—*the substance of the debate as framed by Robertson and the anti-Keynesians*—was concerned with the way in which saving affects the economic system.  As a result, the anti-Keynesians walked away from the debate believing their view of the beneficial role of saving had been vindicated.

This created a situation in which economists have taken positions on both sides of the issue—some arguing that saving inhibits economic growth and employment (demand-side economics) and others arguing that economic growth and employment are stimulated by saving (supply-side economics).  The result has been a rudderless guide to *ad hoc* policies over the past fifty years that have led us to where we find ourselves today, faced with a bitter divide over the appropriate response to the economic, political, and social crisis that has been developing throughout the world since the Crash of 2008—a divide in which neither side seems to be able to understand why the other is so confused.

I believe that given the history of the LP/LF debate this divide cannot be bridged in the absence of a clear understanding of the way in which the rate of interest is determined within the context in which the issue was originally raised by Keynes, namely, within the context of the Marshallian paradigm of supply and demand.  There are many grounds on which one can criticize this paradigm, but I suspect that almost all economists recognize its essential validity, and I can't even imagine what it would be like to try to make sense out of a market economy in a principles course without the concepts of supply and demand as put forth by Marshall.  If we are unable to start with an explanation of the way in which prices and quantities are determined by the actions of decision-making units in individual markets within the context of a Marshallian partial-equilibrium analysis, how is it possible to provide a *causal* explanation of the way in which prices and quantities are determined within any economic model?

It is the purpose of this monograph to sort through the issues of the LP/LF debate in order to provide a definitive explanation of the way in which the rate of interest is determined within the Marshallian paradigm of supply and demand, and, beyond this, to explain the fundamental connection between the central thesis of Keynes' *General Theory—that consumption is the driving force for economic growth and employment, not saving*—and the economic, political, and social problems we face today.

**Chapter I**, **Robertson versus Keynes**, reviews the arguments of the controversy between Robertson and Keynes that are essential to understanding the issues that separated the two sides in the LP/LF debate.  It is argued that whether or not the loanable-funds theory is consistent with the Marshallian paradigm is the seminal issue raised by Keynes in *The General Theory*, but this issue became lost in Robertson's conflation of three separate issues raised by Keynes: 1) whether or not the rate of interest is determined by saving and investment, 2) whether or not an increase in the propensity to save can stimulate the formation of capital, and 3) whether or not full employment can be maintained in the long run by monetary policy alone.

These three issues are examined in detail below, the first in **Chapter II**, **The Theory of Interest**, which explains the causal/dynamic nature of Keynes' theory of interest, and the second and third in **Chapter III**, **The Long-Period Problem of Saving**, which argues that the failure to understand the causal/dynamic nature of Keynes' theory of interest led policy makers to ignore the long-period problem of saving that Keynes' explained throughout *The General Theory*—that is, the problem of maintaining full employment in the long run in the face of a declining prospective yield at the margin due to the increasing stock of capital that results from the flow of saving/investment.

**Chapter IV**, **The Long-Period Problem of Debt**, argues that the failure to appreciate Keynes' long-period problem of saving led to the fundamental problem we face today, namely, what may be referred to as *the long-period problem of debt*—that is, a situation in which the institutions within society are such that, given the state of mass-production technology, the full employment of existing resources can only be achieved and maintained through an unsustainable increase in debt relative to income. It is further argued that the reason we face this problem today is because of the increase in the concentration of income and international imbalances that have occurred over the past thirty-five years that are the result of the *institutional changes* brought on by the economic policies that have been implemented over the past forty-five years.

**Chapter V**, **Concluding Observations**, argues that ignoring Keynes' long-period problem of saving—combined with a failure to understand its companion, the long-period problem of debt—resulted in the adoption of economic policies over the past forty-five years that have taken us down a road that inevitably leads to the kind of financial crisis we experienced in 2008 and the economic stagnation that followed. It is argued that there can be little hope for the future so long as economists are unable to come to a clear understanding of Keynes' long-period problem of saving in a way that leads to an overwhelming consensus within the discipline of economics to the effect that— *consumption is the driving force for economic growth and employment, not saving.*

This book is chiefly addressed to my fellow economists. I hope that it will be intelligible to others. But its main purpose is to deal with difficult questions of theory, and only in the second place with the applications of this theory to practice. For if orthodox economics is at fault, the error is to be found not in the superstructure, which has been erected with great care for logical consistency, but in a lack of clearness and of generality in the premisses. Thus I cannot achieve my object of persuading economists to re-examine critically certain of their basic assumptions except by a highly abstract argument and also by much controversy. I wish there could have been less of the latter. But I have thought it important, not only to explain my own point of view, but also to show in what respects it departs from the prevailing theory. Those, who are strongly wedded to what I shall call 'the classical theory', will fluctuate, I expect, between a belief that I am quite wrong and a belief that I am saying nothing new. It is for others to determine if either of these or the third alternative is right. My controversial passages are aimed at providing some material for an answer; and I must ask forgiveness if, in the pursuit of sharp distinctions, my controversy is itself too keen. I myself held with conviction for many years the theories which I now attack, and I am not, I think, ignorant of their strong points.

John Maynard Keynes
1936

# Chapter I:
# Robertson versus Keynes

*There are none so blind as those who will not see.*
*Thomas Chalkley, 1713*

Keynes explained his theory of interest in Chapter 13 of *The General Theory*:

> The rate of interest is not the "price" which brings into equilibrium the demand for resources to invest with the readiness to abstain from present consumption. It is the "price" which equilibrates the desire to hold wealth in the form of cash with the available quantity of cash;—which implies that if the rate of interest were lower, i.e. if the reward for parting with cash were diminished, the aggregate amount of cash which the public would wish to hold would exceed the available supply, and that if the rate of interest were raised, there would be a surplus of cash which no one would be willing to hold. If this explanation is correct, the quantity of money is the other factor, which, in conjunction with liquidity-preference, determines the actual rate of interest in given circumstances. (1936, pp.167-8)

It is worth noting at the beginning that this is a decidedly Marshallian explanation of the way in which the rate of interest is determined in terms of the supply and demand for money.

In his June 1936 review of *The General Theory*, Hicks argued that there is no fundamental difference between Keynes' theory of interest and the proposition that the rate of interest is determined by the supply and demand for loans since "by mere arithmetic" (p. 236) they amount to the same thing, a sentiment echoed by Robertson in December of that year. Hick's argument is analogous to the role of Walras' Law in a general equilibrium model which makes it possible to ignore any one of the equilibrium conditions in analyzing its properties. According to Hicks' argument, if the loanable-funds equilibrium condition is ignored we are left with the liquidity-preference theory, and if the liquidity-preference equilibrium condition is ignored we are left with the loanable-funds theory. Since we end up with the same set of equilibrium values whichever equilibrium condition we ignore it makes no difference which theory we choose to embrace or ignore. This is a decidedly non-Marshallian view of the way in which the rate of interest is determined.[2]

In March of 1937, Bertil G. Ohlin attempted to explain the Stockholm theory of saving and investment in which a distinction is made between *ex ante* and *ex post* analysis wherein *ex ante* refers to "*anticipated, i.e., expected or planned* income, savings, investment, etc." and *ex post* refers to "realized" results. (p. 64) Then, in June of that year Ohlin argued that these concepts can be used to explain the way in which saving and investment determine the rate of interest by way of the supply and demand for credit. According to Ohlin, "rates of interest are governed by this supply and demand in the usual way," (p. 225) which brings us back to Marshall.

Keynes replied to his critics in June of 1937 and insisted that his and the alternative version of his theory put forth by Hicks, Robertson, and Ohlin are "rad-

---

[2] Lerner's *reductio ad absurdum* response to Hick's argument was to ask: "If...he [Hicks] had eliminated the supply of and demand for peanuts, what then?" (Klein, 1966, p. 118)

ically opposed to one another." (p. 241) He then singled out Ohlin's Marshallian presentation of the *ex ante* loanable-funds version of this alternative theory and observed that Ohlin had defined his terms such that "the net supply and demand of credit are equal *ex definition* whatever interest level exists on the market" and argued that this definition made Ohlin's theory identical to "the classical doctrine...namely, that the rate of interest is fixed at the level where the supply of credit, in the shape of saving is equal to the demand for credit, in the shape of investment." (p. 245) [3] Keynes then explained how his liquidity-preference theory of interest had arisen from the realization that saving and investment determine income, not the rate of interest, and that once it became clear that "the rate of interest is not determined by saving and investment in the same way in which price is determined by supply and demand" he was forced to seek an alternative explanation for the determination of the rate of interest. [4]

---

[3] Ohlin:

> ...*Ex-post* one finds equality between the total quantity of new credit during the period, and the sum total of positive individual savings.... Thus, there is a connection between the rate of interest, which is the price of credit, and the process of economic activity, of which the flow of saving is a part. (June 1937, p. 224)

[4] Keynes:

> Aggregate saving and aggregate investment, in the senses in which I have defined them, are necessarily equal in the same way in which the aggregate purchases of anything on the market are equal to the aggregate sales. But this does not mean that 'buying' and 'selling' are identical terms, and that the laws of supply and demand are meaningless... [The] novelty lies in my maintaining that it is not the rate of interest, but the level of incomes which ensures equality between savings and investment. The arguments which lead up to this initial conclusion are independent of my

In his September 1937 response to Keynes, Ohlin argued that Keynes was confused with regard to the relationship between *ex post* and *ex ante* magnitudes. Ohlin then asserted that anyone who refuses to accept his analysis of the way in which saving and investment determine the rate of interest through the supply and demand for credit "must...refute also the Marshallian supply and demand curve analysis in *toto*."[5] (pp. 425-

---

> subsequent theory of the rate of interest, and in fact I reached it before I had reached the latter theory. But the result of it was to leave the rate of interest in the air. If the rate of interest is not determined by saving and investment in the same way in which price is determined by supply and demand, how is it determined? (1937, pp. 211-12)

And:

> As I have said...the initial novelty lies in my maintaining that it is not the rate of interest, but the level of incomes which ensures equality between saving and investment. The...result...was to leave the rate of interest in the air. If the rate of interest is not de-termined by saving and investment in the same way in which price is determined by supply and demand, how is it determined?The resulting theory, whether right or wrong, is exceedingly simple— namely, that the rate of interest on a loan of given quality and maturity has to be established at the level which, in the opinion of those who have the opportunity of choice—i.e. of wealth-hold-ers—equalizes the attractions of holding idle cash and of holding the loan. (June 1937, p.249-50)

[5] The term *ex ante* as it applies to the LP/LF debate is subject to much confusion in economics. Most economists simply accept Klein's (1966, pp.114-6) ambiguous interpretation of this term to the effect that "*ex ante* quantities are taken to be schedules of economic behavior" (Klein, 1966, p.116) which Klein derived from Ohlin's September 1937 at-tempt to clarify what he meant by this term. But Ohlin continued to de-scribe *ex ante* in terms of what is "planned" (pp. 423-24) in this attemp-ted clarification rather than in terms of what decision-making units are *willing* to do as Marshall had described these schedules throughout his *Principles*. Klein did nothing to clarify this issue. Specifically, Klein did not explain how *planned* saving can affect the economic system in a way that is comparable to the effects of *planned* investment. (See

26)

It is demonstrated in **Chapter II** below that Ohlin's assertion that in order to reject his analysis it is necessary to "refute also the Marshallian supply and demand curve analysis in *toto*" blithely ignored Keynes' demonstration in *A Treatise on Money* that *any* theory that assumes the rate of interest to be determined by saving and investment is inconsistent with the Marshallian supply and demand curve analysis. As we shall see in **Chapter II**, whether or not the loanable-funds theory is consistent with the Marshallian paradigm is the seminal issue with regard to the theory of interest raised by Keynes in his *Treatise on Money* and in *The General Theory*, but this issue became lost in the LP/LF debate by Robertson's framing the debate in terms of what he referred to as the "long-period problem of saving."

### I-a. Robertson's Criticism of Keynes

In his November 1936 review of *The General Theory*, Robertson took Keynes to task for his analysis of what Robertson called "the long-period problem of saving." Since this criticism of Keynes stands at the very center of the controversy between Robertson and Keynes, it is quoted here at length:

> According to Mrs. Robinson,[2] Mr. Keynes' theory "has been developed mainly in terms of short period

---

Keynes [June 1937, 248n], Bibow, Brady, Hayes, and section **II-d** below.) Nor did Klein shed any light on why Ohlin talked in terms of *plans* rather than *willingness* in explaining what he ment by *ex ante*. To avoid confusion, it must be remembered that Keynes used the term *ex ante* exactly as Ohlin explained it in March and June of 1937, that is, to mean something that is "*anticipated, i.e., expected or planned*," and not in the Marshallian sense of *willingness*.

analysis;" but...it may be convenient to conclude by examining briefly the bearing of his "liquidity preference" formula on the long-period problem of saving. This problem can be put in various forms, of which I choose what is, I hope, alike the simplest and the best adapted to bring out Mr. Keynes' points. Will an increased rate of saving which is not itself hoarding (e.g. which takes the form of an increased demand for securities), but which involves an actual diminution in the rate of expenditure on consumable goods, lead to a progressive shrinkage in total money income?

In one of his extremer passages (pp. 211-213) Mr. Keynes appears to invoke his formula in support of the view that such an event has *no* tendency to bring down the rate of interest nor therefore to stimulate the formation of capital equipment. *For why, he asks, the quantity of money being unchanged, should a fresh[3] act of saving diminish the sum which it is required to keep in liquid form at the existing rate of interest?* [emphasis added] The answer surely emerges from the composite nature of "liquidity preference." If the event in question deprives the producers of consumption goods of income, it reduces by the same act their ability to hold money for "transaction" and "precautionary" purposes. It is only if they resist the switch in public demand by continuing to indulge in expenditure, to offer employment, and hence to hold (or cause to be held) money balances on the old scale, that "liquidity preference" as defined will remain unchanged. Mr. Keynes' argument in this passage seems to be *a repetition in disguise of his old argument that increased saving which is not itself hoarding is necessarily balanced by the sale of securities on the part of entrepreneurs who are making losses but are determined not to restrict the amount or change the character of their output* [emphasis added]. In so far as this argument is ever valid, it is as valid when employment is full to start with as when it is not—indeed, as Professor Hayek pointed out long ago,[4] it depends on the assumption that employment will be *kept* full at all costs: it is thus not easy to reconcile with Mr. Keynes' concession to the efficacy of Thrift under conditions of full employment (p. 112). *So long as such a situation exists and is expected to continue, the rate of interest will, it is true, not fall* [*emphasis* added] nor the formation of capital equipment be stimulated, but neither, so far as the mere maintenance of income[5] and employment goes, is it necessary that they should. If such a situation does *not* exist, there is nothing in the doctrine of liquidity preference to invalidate the common-sense view that the increased demand for securities will tend to raise their price.

There remains, however, a further point. Even tho the producers of consumption goods take their medicine, nevertheless, if there exists for the community as a whole a negatively inclined curve of "liquidity preference proper"...some part of the additional savings devoted by individuals to the purchase of securities will come to rest in the banking accounts of those who, at the higher price of securities, desire to hold an increased quantity of money.[6] Thus the fall in the rate of interest and the stimulus to the formation of capital will be less than if [the liquidity-preference curve] were a vertical straight line, and the stream of money income will tend to contract....

It would, I think, be agreed by "orthodox" writers[7] that this is a situation calling for a progressive increase in the supply of money. (1936, pp. 187-8)

In this passage, Robertson clearly states his belief that the only obstacle to maintaining income in the face of an "increased rate of saving" is "the additional savings...come to rest in...banking accounts" that results from the fall in the rate of interest ("higher price of securities"). In Robertson's view of this problem, this is "a situation calling for a progressive increase in the supply of money," hence, a problem that can be easily solved by increasing the supply of money. At the same time, Robertson's explanation of "Mr. Keynes' points" is at odds with what Keynes actually said with regard to these points.

To begin with, Robertson misstated the question asked by Keynes in "one of his extremer passages (pp. 211-213)." Keynes did not ask why the quantity of money being unchanged, should a fresh act of saving diminish the sum which it is "required" to keep in liquid form at the existing rate of interest as Robertson asserted. What Keynes actually asked was why a fresh act of saving should diminish the sum which it "is desired to keep in liquid form at the existing rate of interest." These are entirely different questions.

Keynes' question as to what is "desired" to keep in liquid form at the existing rate of interest has to do with the *demand* for liquidity, that is, the quantity of liquidity *demanded* at the existing rate of interest. Robertson's misstatement as to what "is required to be kept in liquid form" and his answer to his own question that if "the event in question deprives the producers of consumption goods of income, it reduces by the same act their ability to hold money for 'transaction' and 'precautionary' purposes" indicates that Robertson is talking about how a change in income will reduce the transactions and precautionary demands for money and, thereby, free those balances to increase the quantity of liquidity *supplied* as the system adjust to a new point of equilibrium. This has nothing to do with Keynes' question with regard to the *demand* for liquid resources at the existing rate of interest.[6]

Keynes' question appears at the end of section I in Chapter 16 of *The General Theory*, and throughout that section Keynes discusses the effects of the "absurd, though almost universal, idea that an act of individual saving is just as good for effective demand as an act of individual consumption...so that current investment is promoted by individual saving to the same extent as present consumption is diminished." According to Robertson, Keynes' argument in this section "seems to be a repetition...of his old argument" from his *Treatise on Money*. Since this old argument also stands at the very center of the controversy between Robertson and Keynes it is also quoted here at length:

> Before leaving this section it may be well to illustrate further the conclusion stated above, that a fall in the price of consumption-goods due to an excess of saving over investment does not in itself—*if it is unaccompanied by any change in the bearishness or bullishness of the public or in the volume of savings-deposits, or if there are compensating changes in these two factors* [*emphasis* added]—require any opposite change in the price of new investment-goods. For I believe that this conclusion may be accepted by some readers with difficulty.
>
> It follows from the fact that, *on the above assumptions* [*emphasis* added], the total value of the investment-goods (new and old) coming on to the market for purchase out of current savings is always exactly equal to the amount of such savings and is irrespective of the current output of investment-goods. For if the value of

---

[6] See footnote 45 below.

the new investment goods is less than the volume of current savings, entrepreneurs as a whole must be making losses exactly equal to the difference. *These losses, which represent a failure to receive cash up to expectations from sales of current output, must be financed, and the non-receipt of the expected cash receipts must be somehow made good. The entrepreneurs can only make them good either by reducing their own bank deposits or selling some of their other capital assets. The bank-deposits thus released and the securities thus sold are available for, and are exactly equal to, the excess of current savings over the value of new investment* [*emphasis* added].

In the more general case where the public sentiment towards securities or the volume of savings-deposits is changing, then if the extent to which the entrepreneurs have recourse to the expedient of releasing bank-deposits plus the increase in savings-deposits allowed by the banking system just balances the increase in the desire of the public to employ their resources in bank-deposits, there is no reason for any change in the price of securities. *If the former is in excess of the latter, the price of securities will tend to rise and if the latter is in excess of the former, the price of securities will tend to fall* [*emphasis* added]. (1930, pp. 130-1)

Both Robertson and Hayek criticized this argument in 1931, arguing that output must change in this situation.[7] In his 1931 reply to this criticism Keynes

---

[7] The exchange between Keynes and Hayek is a most interesting example of the kind of paradigmatic debate discussed by Kuhn (chs.VIII-XI), as is the entire LP/LF controversy itself. Particular attention should be paid to Keynes' (November 1931) reply to Hayek in this regard, for in this reply Keynes carefully examined the obstacles that arise as a result of the conflicting views of reality embodied in their respective paradigms. See also Keynes (Sept. 1931). Much of *The General Theory* is also devoted to explaining the kinds of paradigmatic differences

restated the argument, and this time he emphasized the words "*in itself*" in the first sentence of the above passage, and toward the end of the discussion he added the following footnote:

> [1]I did not deal in detail in my book, and I am not dealing here, with the train of events which ensues when, as a consequence of making losses, entrepreneurs reduce their output. This is a long story...which I intend to treat in detail in due course. Its only bearing on the present argument is that a change in output affects the demand for active deposits, and may therefore (according to how the banking system behaves) affect the supply of hoards. (September 1931, p. 418)

In addition, in the preface to *The General Theory*, Keynes explained the nature of the theoretical arguments put forth in his *Treatise on Money* as an "instantaneous picture taken on the assumption of a given output." (pp. vi-vii)

From a) Keynes' old argument itself, b) Keynes' emphasis on the words "*in itself*" in his response to Robertson's and Hayek's criticisms, c) Keynes' footnote stating that his argument does not, in fact, deal with the situation in which output changes, and d) Keynes' explanation in the preface to *The General Theory* that his argument in *A Treatise on Money* assumes "a given output," it should be clear that in spite of the fact that Robertson presented his objections to Keynes' old argument within the context of "the long-period problem of saving," Keynes' old argument does not deal with the long-period effects of an increased rate of saving on income or the rate of interest. Spe-

---

discussed by Kuhn.

cifically, it has to do with a *ceteris paribus* situation in which *output is assumed to be constant*. This is, of course, *precisely the kind of ceteris paribus situation that is the essence of Marshall*'s *partial equilibrium methodology.*

What Robertson described in the above passage is not Keynes' long-period problem of savings, that is— the problem of maintaining full employment in the long run in the face of a declining prospective yield at the margin due to the increasing stock of capital that results from saving/investment. The problem Robertson described was what may be called the short-period problem of saving, that is—the problem of achieving full employment in the short run in the face of an increase in the propensity to save.

Robertson's conflation of these two problems and attributing this conflation to Keynes is obviously a straw-man since at no time did Keynes argue that an increased rate of saving can have no effect on income or the rate of interest *over the course of some indefinite period of time* as Robertson's arguments insinuate in the passage quoted above. Nor did Keynes argue that *therefore* (i.e., because of this) an increased rate of saving cannot stimulate the formation of capital. As we shall see in **Chapter II**, and further expound upon in **Chapter III**, Keynes' argued that an increase in the propensity to save will, indeed, lead to a fall in employment, output, income, and the rate of interest *over time*, but Keynes' explanation as to *how* and *why* this will occur is, in fact, "radically opposed" to Robertson's explanation as to *how* and *why* this will occur.

It is demonstrated below that Robertson's supposition that Keynes based his analysis of the "long-period problem of saving" on the assumption that an increase in the propensity to save will not lead to a fall in income and the rate of interest was a red herring in that it conflated two separate issues raised by Keynes: 1) whether or not an increase in the propensity to save can, *in itself*, cause a fall in the rate of interest and 2) whether or not an increase in the propensity to save can stimulate the formation of capital. In addition, Robertson's conclusion that the system can be returned to or kept at full employment through "a progressive increase in the supply of money" is a third, but, again, separate issue raised by Keynes that Robertson conflated with the other two. Keynes disagreed with Robertson on all three of these issues, and all three of these issues are examined in detail below, the first in **Chapter II** and the second and third in **Chapter III**.

### I-b. Where Robertson and Keynes Disagreed

During the course of discussing possible sources of confusion that could arise from Ohlin's having defined *ex ante* investment as investment that is *"anticipated, i.e., expected or planned,"* in June of 1937 Keynes introduced his concept of the demand for 'finance'.[8] In the process, he conceded that a demand

---

[8] Keynes explained his reasons for introducing his concept of 'finance' in a letter to E. S. Shaw dated 13 April, 1938:

> One point I do agree with. I do not consider that the conception of 'finance' makes any really significant change in my previous theory. It is, as you say, no more than a type of active balance which I had not sufficiently emphasized in my book. I described it as 'the coping stone' and attached importance to it in my article mainly because it seemed to me that it provided a bridge between my way of talking and the way of those who discuss the supply of loans and credits etc. I thought it might help to show that they were simply discussing one of the sources of demand for liquid funds

for *money* can arise from *planned* activity and that *planned* activity can have a direct effect on the rate of interest through an effect on the demand for money as money balances are accumulated in anticipation of planned expenditures. Thus, Keynes conceded that *changes* in planned investment can have a direct effect on the rate of interest *to the extent these changes affect the demand for money.* At the same time, he insisted that changes in actual consumption or investment, or in either planned or actual saving, cannot have an effect on the rate of interest independent of its effects on the supply or demand for money. To emphasize this point, in December of that year Keynes emphatically stated: "The investment market can become congested through shortage of cash. It can never become congested through shortage of saving. This is the most fundamental of my conclusions within this field."(p. 669).

In his June 1938 response to Keynes' explanation of the demand for finance, Robertson denied the relevance of this concept and continued to maintain that the two theories are equivalent:

> I am afraid for the moment Mr. Keynes' olive-branch seems to me to add to the methodological confusion. I nourish a hope that he will yet come to agree that analysis in terms of supply and demand for money-to-hold at a moment of time, and analysis in terms of supply

---

arising out of an increase in activity. But, alas, I have only driven them into more tergiversations. I am really driving at something extremely plain and simple which cannot possibly deserve all this exegesis. (Keynes, 1979, p. 282)

Keynes' demand for 'finance' is explained in Blackford (2020, ch. 5) within a formal model that does not conflate stocks and flows.

and demand for money-to-lend during an interval of time, are *alternative* methods of procedure: and that, while neither is more than a first stage in the elucidation of the underlying forces governing the behaviour of the rate of interest, either, *if carried through consistently*, will give the same result as the other. But at present, in attempting to graft on to his old static apparatus such concepts as "the flow of new finance" and "the supply of liquidity," he seems to me to be engaged in breeding a monstrous hybrid between the two methods of approach. (Robertson and J.M.K., June, 1938, p.317)

Robertson then attempted to narrow the issue by considering a case in which an increase in planned investment has led to pressure on the rate of interest to rise through "congestion in the capital market" and asking:

Suppose...the public decide to spend more of their incomes on securities and less on consumable goods. Under what conditions will this decision tend to relieve the congestion in the capital market? Does Mr. Keynes hold that it will have *no* such tendency, unless indeed we happen to be at some rarely attained point described as "full employment"? Or would he agree that in all but very extreme conditions it *will* have such a tendency, and that the conditions postulated in his model—namely, a rising hunger on the part of entrepreneurs for the control of funds—are precisely those in which, even if we are still far from that elusive point of "full employment," this tendency is likely to be important[2]?

If he would agree to this, then his conclusion that "the investment market...can never become congested through short-age of saving" seems to me at best a mere bundle of words, diverting attention from the point of substance—namely, that congestion *would* be relieved by an increase of thrift. But if he would not agree, then there still remains, I think, outstanding between him and his critics, an important issue of substance. (Robertson and J.M.K., June, 1938, p.318)

In his response to this criticism Keynes agreed that a reduction in consumption will relieve the congestion in the capital market *if it leads to a reduction in the demand for money by way of a fall in income.*[9] But Keynes did not agree his claim that "the investment market...can never become congested through shortage of saving" is a "mere bundle of words," and he added:

It is Mr. Robertson's incorrigible confusion between the revolving fund of money in circulation and the flow of new saving which causes all his difficulties. *Saving has no special efficacy, as compared with consumption, in releasing cash and restoring liquidity* [*emphasis* added].... A given level of activity and income will involve the same active demand for cash...irrespective of the current rate of net investment and saving—irrespective indeed of whether there is any investment and saving.... In short, I accept the usual view that the demand for cash in the active circulation is a function of income and of business habits,

---

[9] Keynes:

My answer to Mr. Robertson's question on p. 318 is, I hope, fairly obvious in the light of what I have already written. The congestion in the capital market can only be relieved by something which reduces the demand or increases the supply of cash.... If the reduction in consumption posited by Mr. Robertson leaves aggregate income unchanged, there is no reason to suppose that it will reduce the demand for cash or relieve the congestion. If, however, it leads to a reduction in income, the resulting diminution in the demand for cash would help to relieve the congestion.... (Robertson and J.M.K., June, 1938, p.321)

not of saving. *The "finance," or cash, which is tied up in the interval between planning and execution, is released in due course after it has been paid out in the shape of income, whether the recipients save it or spend it* [*emphasis* added].... Until Mr. Robertson understands that, he will not grasp what I am driving at, however carefully I attempt to reword it. (Robertson and J.M.K., June, 1938, pp. 321-2)

Keynes' comments in the above passages brought the controversy between Robertson and Keynes to a head as it elicited the following reply from Robertson:

In drafting a reply to Mr. Keynes's comments, I wrote as follows: "Nevertheless, I must thank Mr. Keynes for rightly intuiting what question I was trying...to ask him: nor is his answer unsatisfactory. For he agrees that normally, and not merely at these rare moments of full employment, an increase of thrift will tend to lower the rate of interest." Mr. Keynes, after reading this sentence, asked me to state that "[sic] if 'an increase of thrift' means, not an increase of savings but 'an increase of thriftiness' (i.e. a decrease in the propensity to consume), and if 'normally' means that the attendant circumstances are such that the increase of thriftiness leads to a recession in employment and in income, but not to any increase in the desire to hold liquid resources, and that the stock of money is constant, *then* he not only agrees with the proposition but claims to have been the first to have stated it in this form."[*sic*]

This statement I am most glad to quote: for I have previously argued (*Quarterly Journal of Economics*, Nov.1936, p.187) that some such proposition concerning the effect of an increase of thrift on the rate of interest can be established with the aid of the apparatus used in Mr. Keynes's book. My difficulty was to find any such proposition in the book itself. Indeed, from certain crucial passages thereof[1] I derived a strong impression that Mr. Keynes's thesis was that, except in conditions of full employment, there existed no route through which an increased desire to save could lower the rate of interest, or—therefore—promote investment.

I must not be understood to accept all the implications about the mechanism and timing of events conveyed in Mr. Keynes's statement quoted above. But it is, I think, something that we are agreed that, from an increase in the desire to save to a fall in the rate of interest, a causal route does, *ceteris paribus*, exist. (Sept., 1938, pp. 555-6)

This reply clearly indicates the extent of the fundamental disagreement between the two men. There is no reason to conclude from the statement of 'agreement' in this passage that Keynes had made a concession to Robertson as to the efficacy of thriftiness in promoting investment, nor is there any reason to conclude that Robertson and Keynes had reached an accord on the efficacy of monetary policy. There is no mention of the relationship between the demand for finance and the demand for credit or of the relationship between the revolving fund of money in circulation and the flow of new saving. An agreement as to the relationship between Keynes' and Robertson's "methods of approach" is conspicuously absent, and even though Robertson is "most glad to quote" Keynes' statement, the first sentence of the last paragraph of Robertson's reply is a clear repudiation of Keynes' statement. A careful reading of Robertson's reply indicates that the only thing on which the two men could have possibly agreed (other than that an increase in thriftiness will lead to a fall in the rate of interest over time which Keynes always believed and never denied) is that Robertson was *wrong* in his interpretation of "certain crucial passages" in *The General Theory*, though, in the face of Robertson's obstinance, there is no reason to believe that Robertson would have even agreed with this.

As we shall see in **Chapter III**, Robertson did not respond in this passage to the fundamental issue raised by Keynes in *The General Theory* with regard to the effects of an increase in saving on the formation of capital or with regard to the efficacy of monetary policy. In fact, throughout his controversy with Keynes and beyond Robertson was dismissive of Keynes' analysis of these issues. And, yet, these differences had virtually no effect on Robertson for in his 1940 summary of the relationship between his and Keynes' theories of interest Robertson concluded:

> …when we have picked our way through these verbal tangles we are left, I think, in no doubt about the relation between the two methods of approach. Essentially they are two different ways of saying the same thing. Mr. Keynes' long-maintained determination to treat them as "radically opposed"…has been to me from the beginning the most baffling feature of this whole controversy. (1940, p.9)

There is a certain irony in this conclusion for in a very real sense "the most baffling feature of this whole controversy" is Robertson's insistence that his and Keynes' methods of approach "are two different ways of saying the same thing." Robertson maintained this position throughout in spite of the fact that his and Keynes' methods of approach were so "radically opposed" that there was virtually nothing on which the two men could agree. When one does pick through the "verbal tangles," as we shall do below, and examines exactly what it is that the two men actually said it becomes clear that they did not say the same thing. Yet, it was literally impossible for Robertson to accept this fact in spite of the extent of his disagreement with what Keynes actually said.

As we shall see, part of the reason for this arose from Robertson's inability to understand, or unwillingness to accept what Keynes' actually said with regard to the relationship between expectations, output, and income in the analytic framework developed by Keynes throughout *The General Theory*.

## I-c. Expectations, Output, and Income

Robertson used the terms "income" and "income received" interchangeably, and by these terms he meant quite literally money received from the sale of output. Thus, Robertson defined income in such a way that the value of income depends only on *the value of output sold*.[10]

Keynes took great care in constructing his definition of income as being equal to sales less user cost, where user cost "is the measure of what has been sacrificed (one way or another) to produce [sales]." (1936, p. 53-4) The fact that this "sacrifice" is, by definition, inversely related to changes in inventories and "maintenance and improvement" means that Keynes defined income as being equal to *the value of output produced*.[11]

The significance of this difference between Rob-

---

[10] See Robertson (Sept. 1933, pp. 401-2; December 1933, pp. 710-1; 1936, p. 171) and cf. Hawtrey (pp. 702, 704) quoted at the end of this section.

[11] See Keynes (1936, pp. 52-5, 63).

ertson's and Keynes' definitions of income can be seen by examining Keynes' explanation of the way in which employment and output produced are determined in his general theory:

> All production is for the purpose of ultimately satisfying a consumer. Time usually elapses, however—and sometimes much time—between the incurring of costs by the producer (with the consumer in view) and the purchase of the output by the ultimate consumer. Meanwhile the entrepreneur...has to form the best expectations[1] he can as to what the consumers will be prepared to pay when he is ready to supply them (directly or indirectly) after the elapse of what may be a lengthy period; and he has no choice but to be guided by these expectations, if he is to produce at all by processes which occupy time.
>
> These expectations, upon which business decisions depend, fall into two groups.... The first type is concerned with the price which a manufacturer can expect to get for his "finished" output at the time when he commits himself to starting the process which will produce it.... The second type is concerned with what the entrepreneur can hope to earn in the shape of future returns if he purchases (or, perhaps, manufactures) "finished" output as an addition to his capital equipment. We may call the former *short-term expectation* and the latter *long-term expectation*.
>
> Thus the behaviour of each individual firm in deciding its daily[1] output will be determined by its *short-term expectations*—expectations as to the cost of output on various possible scales and expectations as to the sale-proceeds of this output.... *It is upon these various expectations that the amount of employment which the firms offer will depend* [*emphasis* added]. The *actually realised* results of the production and sale of output *will only be relevant to employment in so far as*

*they cause a modification of subsequent expectations* [*emphasis* added]. Nor, on the other hand, are the original expectations relevant, which led the firm to acquire the capital equipment and the stock of intermediate products and half-finished materials with which it finds itself at the time when it has to decide the next day's output. *Thus, on each and every occasion of such a decision, the decision will be made, with reference indeed to this equipment and stock, but in the light of the current expectations of prospective costs and sale-proceeds* [*emphasis* added]. (1936, pp.46-7)

Thus, Keynes argued that whenever production takes time, at each and every point in time at which a decision must be made concerning employment and output that decision must be made with reference to existing capital equipment on the basis of currently held *expectations* with regard to the costs to be paid and the proceeds to be received in the *future* while the output is being produced and when it is to be sold. The actual costs and proceeds that result from employment and output decisions cannot have a direct effect on these decisions, only an indirect effect, and, even then, only to the extent they have an effect on stocks of capital assets and *subsequent* expectations, that is, on the capital stocks that exist and expectations formed *after* the expected costs and proceeds are (or are not) actually realized.[12] This argument has

---

[12] Keynes:

> It is evident from the above that the level of employment at any time depends, in a sense, not merely on the existing state of expectation but on the states of expectation which have existed over a certain past period. Nevertheless past expectations, which have not yet worked themselves out, are embodied in the to-day's capital equipment with reference to which the entrepreneur has to make to-day's decisions, and only influence his decisions in so far as

a clear implication with regard to income.

As was noted above, Keynes constructed his definition of income in such a way that income is equal to the value of output *produced.* Whenever production takes time, income, so defined, is earned (accrues) *before* the output produced in generating income is sold. This makes income a psychological phenomenon in Keynes' general theory, determined in the minds of decision-making units, and *this value cannot be separated from the expectations of these units.* The implication is that *whenever production takes time*, at each and every point in time at which a decision must be made concerning income, that decision must be made on the basis of currently held expectations just as the corresponding decisions concerning the employment and output that generates that income must be made on the basis of currently held expectations.[13]

The relationship between employment, output, income, and the entrepreneurs' *expectations* is stated explicitly by Keynes in his definition of effective demand:

> Furthermore, the *effective demand* is simply the aggregate income (or proceeds) which the entrepreneurs *expect* [*emphasis* added] to receive, inclusive of the incomes which they will hand on to the other factors of production, from the amount of current employment which they decide to give. The aggregate demand function relates various hypothetical quantities of em-

---

they are so embodied. It follows, therefore, that, in spite of the above, to-day's employment can be correctly described as being governed by to-day's expectations taken in conjunction with to-day's capital equipment. (1936, p. 50)

[13] See Keynes (1936, chs. 5-6).

ployment to the proceeds which their outputs are *expected* [*emphasis* added] to yield; and the effective demand is the point on the aggregate demand function which becomes effective because, taken in conjunction with the conditions of supply, it corresponds to the level of employment which maximises the entrepreneur's *expectation* [*emphasis* added] of profit. (1936, p. 55)

Effective demand as defined in terms of the *proceeds* producers *expect* to receive as they maximize their *expectation* of profits through the employment of resources is assumed to be the *direct* determinant of employment, output, and, hence, *income* in Keynes' general theory, and the importance of the psychological dependence of income on expectations is emphasized again by Keynes in his discussion of the relationship between *net* income and consumption.

In defining *net* income, Keynes adjusted gross income (i.e., the value of output produced) for all of those factors that are either "voluntary" (e.g., user cost) or if not voluntary at least "not unexpected" (i.e., supplementary costs), and he explicitly excluded consideration of those factors that are "unforeseen" (i.e., windfalls). (1936, p. 57-8) By defining net income in this way Keynes was able to draw a distinction (at least conceptually) between the way in which net income (defined in terms of *expected* and *not unexpected* results) and windfalls (defined in terms of *unexpected* results) affect decision-making behavior with regard to consumption.[14]  Thus, decisions con-

---

[14] See Keynes (1936, ch. 6). It is worth noting the importance of expectation is implicit in Keynes' definition of income in the *Treatise* where income is assumed to include "normal remuneration" and exclude "profits" or "windfalls" (see Keynes, 1930, Chapter 9). The con-

cerning consumption in Keynes' general theory are made with reference to existing wealth (i.e., "capital account") on the basis of *currently held expectations* with regard to net income.

The psychological dependence of decisions concerning employment, output, income, and consumption on expectations is of the utmost importance in Keynes' general theory for it is the psychological dependence of decisions on *expectations* that provides the distinction between the way in which expected and realized results affect decision-making behavior: Expectations affect *current* decisions directly whether they are realized in the future or not while realized results only affect decisions made *after* the results are (or are not) actually realized. This distinction lies at the very core of Keynes' view of casualty for it determines *the temporal order in which events must occur* which makes it possible to separate cause and effect.

---

cept (as opposed to the definition) of income employed by Keynes in *The General Theory* is, to a large extent, the same as the concept of income employed by Keynes in the *Treatise* (see Keynes, 1936, pp.77-8). Keynes did not attempt to provide an operational definition for his concept of income, and no attempt shall be made to do so here except to note that I see no fundamental inconsistency between Keynes' theoretical construct and Friedman's (1957) permanent income hypothesis. I find this hypothesis to fit fairly well within the context of Keynes' general theory *as it relates to the equilibrium properties of Keynes' model* where the distinction between expected and realized results defines the circumstances in which the system is equilibrium, namely, when expectations are realized and windfalls do not occur. Friedman's formulation does seem to be somewhat lacking, however, when it comes to accounting for the effect of windfalls on consumption in that Keynes did not assume that net income was the sole factor in determining consumption: "This is not, of course, the only factor of which he takes account when he is deciding how much to spend. It makes a *considerable* [emphasis added] difference, for example, how much windfall gain or loss he is making on capital account." (1936, p. 58)

*It is the ability to separate cause and effect that makes a causal analysis of dynamic behavior possible in Keynes' general theory.*

When income is defined as Keynes defined it the causally significant variable becomes the value of output produced *as perceived by decision-making units in light of their current expectations.* This value is equal to Robertson's definition of income as the value of output sold changes randomly over time only if expectations are unit-elastic and the value of output produced adjusts *instantaneously* to changes in sales. But whether expectations and the value of output produced are determined in this way or not, the value of output produced as perceived by decision-making units depends on their current expectations in Keynes' general theory, and, *given the level of employment and output*, income cannot change except through a change in expectations.

When income is defined as Robertson defined it such that its value is equal to the value of output sold, income becomes an *ex-post* variable the value of which is determined *after* output is sold. Thus, *Robertson's definition of income does not allow for the distinction that is central to Keynes' view of causality*—namely, the distinction between the way in which expected and realized results affect decision-making behavior with regard to employment, output, income, and consumption. As we shall see, it is the absence of this distinction that limits Robertson's methodology to that of comparative-statics.[15]

---

[15] It is worth noting that expectations play a central role in separating cause and effect throughout Marshall's *Principles*, a fact that Hicks (1946, p. 117) identifies with Marshall's dynamic methodology. It

In December 1933, Ralph G. Hawtrey attempted to explain the importance of the psychological dependence of income on expectations to Robertson:

> The relation between income and expenditure is a psychological one; the recipient of income regulates his expenditure by his receipts. And it is by no means true that the disposal of income, interpreted in this sense, only occurs at an interval after receipt. Indeed it is more often true that expenditure on consumption is regulated with reference to *future* income than to past income. The purpose of a cash balance is to permit of expenditure being in some degree independent of receipts. It is a capital fund, and, in deciding what drafts to make upon it, the owner considers primarily what his future current receipts are likely to be. (p. 702)

And further on:

> ...it is theoretically *possible* so to adjust prices that there is no change in stocks of goods. But why does Mr. Robertson persist in adopting this hypothesis? It is utterly out of accord with the facts of practical life. It implies that retail prices are exactly and instantaneously adjusted to any change in demand *every day*. The introduction of so extravagant an assumption places all

---

should also be noted that this distinction marks a fundamental difference between Keynes' *Treatise on Money* and *The General Theory*. In Chapter 7 of *The General Theory* Keynes observed that in his "*Treatise on Money* the concept of *changes* in the excess of investment over saving, as there defined, was a way of handling changes in profit, though I did not in that book distinguish clearly between expected and realised results[1.]" (p. 77) In the accompanying footnote he noted that his "method [in the *Treatise*] was to regard the current realised profit as determining the current expectation of profit." Thus, while Keynes did not distinguish between expected and realized results in the *Treatise*, he decidedly made this distinction in *The General Theory* where he explicitly renounced the implicit assumption of unit-elastic expectations of the *Treatise*.

his analysis on an abstract plane from which it cannot be redeemed till the assumption is modified. (p.704)

Robertson responded that he found his own formulation to be "easier than Mr. Hawtrey's conception of consumers' outlay, which is defined as expenditure 'out of income' though the income which it is 'out of' may apparently not yet have been received." (Dec. 1933, p. 711) Robertson was simply unable to grasp the essential nature and validity of the point Hawtrey was attempting to make, namely, that, in the real world, expenditures are determined by *expectations* ("with reference to *future* income") and are not *causally* determined by *realized* income as defined by sales.

That herein lies the fundament difference between Robertson's and Keynes' methods of analysis—Keynes' method being *causal* and *dynamic* and Robertson's method being *descriptive* and *static*—can be seen by contrasting Robertson's and Keynes' understanding of the way in which the effects of an increase in saving, that is, an increase in the propensity to save, work their way through the economic system *through time*, given Robertson's and Keynes' respective definitions of income.

### I-d. The Static Nature of Robertson's Analysis

Robertson's understanding of the way in which the effects of an increase in saving work their way through the system through time, along with his understanding of Keynes' analysis of this process, can be found in Robertson's 1936 review of *The General Theory* quoted in section **I-a** above, also in his attempt to explain the relationship between his and Keynes' theories of interest in Robertson's 1940 *Essays* (pp. 18-9), and again in his 1959 *Lectures* (pp. 67-70). The following passage is from his 1940 *Essays*:

> Let me state in my own language what I believe the Keynesian is trying to convey. Suppose that I decide to spend £100 of my income on securities, instead of as hitherto on fine clothes. My action destroys £100 of the income of my tailor and his employees and depletes their money balances by £100. It also raises the price of securities, i.e. lowers the rate of interest.[3] This fall in the rate of interest tempts some people to sell securities and to hold increased money balances instead. Thus the fall in the rate of interest is checked, and not all of my £100 succeeds therefore in finding its way through the markets for old securities and new issues, on to the markets for labor and commodities. Thus owing to the existence of this siding or trap, my act of thrift does not succeed, as "classical" theory asserts that it will, in creating incomes and money balances for builders and engineers equal to those which it has destroyed for tailors. The net result of the whole proceeding is a fall in the rate of interest and an increase, perhaps, in capital outlay[1] but a net decrease in the total of money incomes and (probably) of employment.
>
> The argument is formally perfectly valid; and the practical inference that, if existing money is going to ground in this way, it is *prima facie* the duty of the banking system to create more money.... Here I will only say that it seems to me a most misleading way of expressing the causal train of events to say, as is sometimes done, that the act of thrift lowers the rate of interest through lowering total incomes. *I should say that it lowers the rate of interest quite directly through swelling the money stream of demand for securities; that this fall in the rate of interest increases the proportion of resources over which people wish to keep command in monetary form; and that this increase in turn is a cause of there being a net decline in total*

*money income,* [*emphasis* added]  i.e. of money incomes not expanding in one sector to the extent that they are contracting in the other.[1] (1940, pp. 18-9)

In this passage Robertson clearly argued that an increase in the propensity to save accompanied by an increase in the purchase of securities ("spend...on securities, instead of...on fine clothes") will have a direct effect on the rate of interest by "swelling the money stream of demand for securities" and that the induced hoarding ("resources...people wish to keep...in monetary form") brought about by the subsequent fall in the rate of interest is "a cause of there being a net decline in total money income." It should be noted that this explanation is dynamic and is explicitly stated in causal terms. At the same time, Robertson's explanation of what Keynes was trying to convey clearly indicates the extent to which Robertson was unable to understand or, perhaps, simply unwilling to address what Keynes was trying to convey.

Keynes did not argue that an increase in saving "destroys... income" or that such an event "also raises the price of securities." As should be clear from the way in which Keynes defined income (and as is explained in detail in **Chapter II** and **Chapter III** below) Keynes argued that an increase in saving only destroys sales, and if the increase in saving persists it will thereby set in motion a *causal chain of events* that must eventually lead to a change in expectations, income, and the rate of interest *over time*. In Keynes' view, an increase in saving cannot have an effect on income until *after* a change in expectations is brought about. By virtue of his old argument from the *Treatise*, in the absence of a change in expectations and a subsequent fall in income the "swelling money stream of demand for securities" that results from the increase in saving must be met by an equal swelling stream of supply of securities caused by the concomitant fall in sales that forces producers of consumption goods to borrow or sell assets in order to obtain the *money* needed to maintain their transactions and precautionary balances as these balances are expended over time. The rate of interest cannot change in response to an increase in saving in this *ceteris paribus* situation until *after* expectations change and the demands for transactions and precautionary balances fall as a *result* of a fall in employment, output, and income.

Robertson's explanation of the way in which an increase in saving affects income and the rate of interest also clearly indicates the extent to which Keynes and Robertson did not say the same thing. For what does it mean to say that an increase in saving "lowers the rate of interest quite directly through swelling the money stream of demand for securities" if Keynes is right, and, *given expectations, income, and the supply and demand for money, this swelling stream of demand must be met by an equal swelling stream of supply?* Why is it "a most misleading way of expressing the causal chain of events to say...the act of thriftiness lowers the rate of interest through lowering total incomes" if Keynes is right, and *the only way in which the rate of interest can fall in this situation is, in fact, after there is a change in expectations that leads to a subsequent fall in employment, output, and, hence, income?*

When we look at what Robertson and Keynes actually said it becomes obvious that they did not say the same thing, and their differences are far from trivial within the analytical framework of Keynes' general theory. Robertson argued that the increase in the supply of loanable funds accompanying an increase in thriftiness can be considered the *direct cause* of the resulting fall in the rate of interest. Keynes argued that only a change in expectations can *cause* a fall in income in this situation, and, as is explained in **Chapter II** below, when income falls it will *cause* a fall in the transactions demand for money which, in turn, will increase the supply of speculative balances which will *cause* the rate of interest to fall *after* income has fallen. These two views of causality are simply irreconcilable within Keynes' general theory, and to reject Keynes' view of causality is to reject Keynes' general theory itself. There is no middle ground on this issue, and not only is it obvious that Keynes and Robertson did not say the same thing concerning this issue, it is also obvious that *if Keynes is right, Robertson is wrong*.

What is not obvious is why anyone would suppose that Keynes is not right. After all, decision-making units do, in fact, live in a world of uncertainty in which production takes time and in which sales fluctuate from day to day, week to week, and month to month. Decision-making units cannot *know* that a fall in sales on any given day or during any given week or month is permanent and will not be compensated for by an increase on the following day or during the following week or month. They are in fact forced to form expectations with various degrees of confidence as to what the future will bring, and their decisions with regard to employment, output, and income must be based on these expectations. Where did Keynes go wrong in assuming that *until expectations change and employment, output, and income fall* decision-making units must sell assets or turn to the credit market to finance their income payments and other contractual payment obligations to the extent these payments cannot be finance otherwise?

Keynes is right, and the point at which Robertson went wrong can be seen by examining footnote 3 at the end of the fourth sentence of Robertson's explanation quoted above:

> [3] Debate on this matter has sometimes been hampered by the ghost of an old argument, dating from the days of the *Treatise on Money*. According to this argument the loss-making tailor, in order to avoid restricting either his personal consumption or the scale of his business, will sell securities to the same amount as I buy them. Obviously, *so long as such a situation continues, the rate of interest will not fall nor the formation of capital equipment be stimulated* [*emphasis* added]; but neither, so far as the mere maintenance of total income (other than the tailor's) and employment goes, is it necessary that they should. Evidently, however, this can only be a *transitional situation* [*emphasis* added] and it is not instructive to stop short at it. (1940, p. 18n)

In this footnote Robertson admitted that Keynes' "old argument" provides a correct analysis of the "transitional situation" under discussion. He then continued his *dynamic* explanation of the way in which the rate of interest is determined in the text and *completely ignored this transitional situation.* But this "transitional situation" has to do with the way in which the system moves *through time.* The only way this transitional situation can be ignored within the context of Keynes' general theory is if it is assumed that expectations are unit-elastic and along with the value of output produced adjust *instantaneously* to changes in sales. If this is not the case *there is no way to explain why firms would be willing to sell at a loss today or reduce their current scale of operations if their expectations are unchanged to the effect that they can accumulate inventories and otherwise maintain their current scale of operations today and expect to sell at a profit tomorrow.* There is no way to make sense out of Robertson's *dynamic* explanation of the way an increase in saving affects the economic system *through time* within the context of Keynes' general theory other than by way of the assumption of unit-elastic expectations with an *instantaneous* adjustment of the value of output produced for *in the absence of this assumption the value of output produced as perceived by decision-making units cannot be equal to the value of output sold as sales change randomly over time.*[16]

This assumption limits Robertson's method of analysis to that of comparative statics in that Robertson's methodology assumes that expectations adjust *instantaneously* in such a way as to achieve a state of static equilibrium *each period* with regard to the determination of income and the rate of interest. He then *describes* how he believes these states of *static* equilibrium will change from period to period. Since

---

[16] Others who have attempted to rationalize Robertson's methodology (e.g., Tsiang, Horwich, and Kohn) are also hobbled by Robertson's implicit unit-elastic, instantaneous adjustment assumption. At no point do those who have attempted to justify Robertson's methodology explain why they believe firms are willing to sell at a loss today if their *expectations* are unchanged to the effect that they can accumulate inventories and otherwise maintain their scale of operations today and *expect* to sell at a profit tomorrow.

Robertson explicitly denied the relevance of Keynes' "transitional situation" to his analysis of the way in which his intraperiod equilibriums are achieved, his dynamic explanation of the way in which an increase in thriftiness affects income and the rate of interest *within each period* is purely *ad hoc* and is irrelevant to the fundamental issue of causality raised by Keynes.[17]

That Robertson's dynamic explanation ignores the fundamental issue of *causality* raised by Keynes is clear in Robertson's footnote quoted above. In this footnote Robertson admitted that if "the loss-making tailor" attempts to avoid "restricting either his personal consumption or the scale of his business" by selling "securities to the same amount as I buy them. ... Obviously...the rate of interest will not fall." What Robertson admitted here is the obvious fact that *in-*

---

[17] This same criticism applies to Hicks' (1946) IS/LM approach to this problem. Hicks, as with Robertson, assumed that the rate of interest and the values of other variables are determined simultaneously within a "week" by a system of equations rather than by the state of supply and demand in the individual markets for debt instruments at any given point in time during the week. It is also worth noting that Hicks explicitly acknowledged this:

> Even when we have mastered the 'working' of the temporary equilibrium system, we are even yet not in a position to give an account of the process of price-change, nor to examine the ulterior consequences of changes in data. These are the ultimate things we want to know about, though we may have to face the disappointing conclusion that there is not much which can be said about them in general. Still, nothing can be done about these further problems until after we have investigated the working of the economy during a particular week. (1946, p. 246)

Hicks' approach to this problem (or lack thereof) as it relates to the difference between Keynes' and Hicks' (i.e., 'Keynesian') methodology is examined in detail in Blackford (2020).

*come and the demand for money must fall* in this situation *before* the rate of interest can fall. Robertson admitted this simple fact on at least four separate occasions[18] without any indication that he understood what this simple fact means with regard to his assertion that his act of saving "lowers the rate of interest quite directly." What this simple fact means is that *it is impossible for an increase in thriftiness to affect the rate of interest directly*. There must be a change in expectations that leads to a fall in income that is accompanied by a fall in the demand for money *before* the rate of interest can fall in this situation.

Once Robertson's analysis is seen to be that of comparative statics it is clear that Robertson's arguments are *irrelevant* to the issues of *causality* raised by Keynes. It is important to understand, however, that Keynes' fundamental objection to the classical theory of interest goes far beyond Robertson's comparative-static exposition of this theory.

---

[18] See Robertson (1936, p. 178; Sept. 1937, p. 435n; 1940, p. 18; 1959, p. 68-9). On each of these occasions Robertson acknowledged the validity of Keynes' old argument.

# Chapter II:
# The Theory of Interest

It is clear that Keynes believed the rate of interest is determined in the credit markets by the supply and demand for loans and debt instruments. He explicitly stated this in *The General Theory* in his discussion of Marshall's treatment of the rate of interest:

> …the equality between the stock of capital-goods offered and the stock demanded will be brought about by the prices of capital-goods, not by the rate of interest. It is equality between the demand and supply of loans of money, i.e. of debts, which is brought about by the rate of interest. (1936, p. 186n)

It is even possible to express Keynes' theory of interest in terms of the supply and demand for loans and debt if one wishes,[19] but it does not follow from this that Keynes' liquidity-preference theory can be viewed as an "alternative version of" the loanable-funds theory or that the liquidity-preference theory "is not as revolutionary as it seems."

It is the notion that saving and investment are brought into equilibrium by adjustments in the rate of interest—that is, that the rate of interest is "determined by saving and investment in the same way in

---

[19] This is in fact done in the model of Keynes' liquidity-preference theory specified in Blackford (2020, ch. 5) wherein it is assumed that firms and households "borrow only to meet their financial needs for *money* and lend only to dispose of excess *money* balances they have no use for otherwise." Accordingly, the supply and demand for loanable funds are specifically defined in terms of the supply and demand for the *stock* of money, and *not* in terms of the *flow* of saving or investment.

which price is determined by supply and demand"
(June 1937, p. 250)—to which Keynes objected, not to
the idea that the rate of interest is determined by supply and demand in the markets for loans and debt.

Keynes' objection to those who argued the equivalence of the two theories is to be found in the fact that,
when formulated within the classical tradition, the
loanable-funds theory is *assumed* to imply the rate of
interest adjusts to equate saving and investment in
such a way that changes in saving or investment can
have no effect on the level of employment, output, or
income. It is simply *assumed* in the classical tradition
that a change in either saving or investment must lead
to a change in the rate of interest that, through its effects on investment, will lead to a change in the *com-
position* of output while leaving aggregate employment, output, and income unchanged.[20]

Keynes saw clearly that it is impossible for savers
and investors to affect the rate of interest in this way
since the rate of interest cannot change in response to

---

[20] See Keynes:

> Certainly the ordinary man—banker, civil servant or politician—
> brought up on the traditional theory, and the trained economist
> also, has carried away with him the idea that whenever an in-
> dividual performs an act of saving he has done something which
> automatically brings down the rate of interest, that this auto-
> matically stimulates the output of capital, and that the fall in the
> rate of interest is just so much as is necessary to stimulate the
> output of capital to an extent which is equal to the increment of
> saving; and, further, that this is a self-regulatory process of adjust-
> ment which takes place without the necessity for any special
> intervention or grandmotherly care on the part of the monetary
> authority. Similarly—and this is an even more general belief, even
> to-day—each additional act of investment will necessarily raise the
> rate of interest, if it is not offset by a change in the readiness to
> save. (1936, p. 177)

an increase in saving until *after* there has been a decrease in income that reduces the demand for money. This means that the rate of interest cannot be determined by saving and investment in the same way price is determined by supply and demand.[21]

But if "the rate of interest is not determined by saving and investment in the same way price is determined by supply and demand, how is it determined?" (Keynes, June 1937, p. 250) To answer this question, Keynes developed his liquidity-preference theory which "makes the rate of interest depend on the present supply of money and the demand schedule for a present claim on money in terms of a deferred claim on money." (June 1937, p. 241)

As a result, Keynes liquidity-preference theory is fundamentally different from that envisioned in the classical tradition irrespective of whether the classical theory is formulated in terms of savings and investment or in terms of the supply and demand for loana-

---

[21] Keynes saw this as a serious mistake, not simply because the theory is inconsistent with the Marshallian paradigm of supply and demand, but because it leads to harmful economic policies:

> The reader will readily appreciate that the problem here under discussion is a matter of the most fundamental theoretical significance and of overwhelming practical importance. For the economic principle, on which the practical advice of economists has been almost invariably based, has assumed, in effect, that, *cet. par.,* a decrease in spending will tend to lower the rate of interest and an increase in investment to raise it. But if what these two quantities [i.e., saving and investment] determine is, not the rate of interest, but the aggregate volume of employment, then our outlook on the mechanism of the economic system will be profoundly changed. A decreased readiness to spend will be looked on in quite a different light if, instead of being regarded as a factor which will, *cet. par.*, increase investment, it is seen as a factor which will, *cet. par.*, diminish employment. (1936, pp. 184-5)

ble funds. In the classical tradition, the rate of interest is *assumed* to adjust to equate saving and investment in either case. In Keynes' theory, the rate of interest is assumed to adjust to equalize "the advantages of holding actual cash and a deferred claim on cash," (June 1937, p. 245) that is, to equate the supply and demand for money (i.e., liquidity).

The difference between the two theories becomes particularly obvious when one compares the difference between the *causal* explanations of the way in which the two theories predict how a change in saving will affect the rate of interest *through time.* While it may appear there are two paradigms in economics in which it is possible to make this comparison, namely, the Walrasian and the Marshallian, in fact, this comparison is only possible within the Marshallian paradigm. The reason it is impossible to make this comparison within the Walrasian paradigm has a direct bearing on the fundamental issue that separated Keynes from his protagonists in the LP/LF debate.

## II-a. Walras, Marshall, and Causality

The reason it is impossible to make this comparison within the Walrasian paradigm arises from the fact that the Walrasian budget constraint assumes the choices of decision-making units are made *simultaneously* at a point in time and are constrained by realized income. This may be the way in which *budgets* are created in the real world, but it is not the way in which *choices* are made. Real-world choices are made *sequentially through time*, not *simultaneously at a point in time*, and neither households nor firms are *constrained* in their choices by income, realized or otherwise, *at the point in time at which a choice must be made.*

The real-world choices of decision-making units are constrained by a) the value and liquidity of their assets, b) the availability of sellers of goods and assets at various prices, c) the availability of buyers of goods and assets at various prices, and d) by their access to credit. The *rate* at which decision-making units receive or earn income *at the point in time at which a choice must be made* has no way of affecting that choice other than through its effects on expectations as anyone who has purchased a home, a car, or has simply walked the aisles of a supermarket knows implicitly, and as any business owner who has had to meet a payroll knows implicitly as well. Decision-making units have no alternative but to be guided by their *expectations* with regard to the income they *expect* to receive in the future and are constrained by the way in which the income they have received in the past has affected the stock of assets they hold in the present, as Keynes insisted (1936, pp. 46-7, 50), but at the point in time at which a choice must be made they are not *constrained* by the *rate* at which they actually receive or earn income in the present or in the future.

Even though the Walrasian budget constraint is called a "constraint" it does not actually constrain the choices of decision-making units.[22]  As a result, the only situation in which this constraint is relevant is when decision-making units and the system as a whole are in a state of static equilibrium. It has no relevance when the system is not in a state of static equilibrium, and even when the system is in a state of static equilibrium the Walrasian budget constraint is little more than an accounting identity that makes it

---

[22] See Clower (1965), Jaffe, Blackford (1975; 1976).

possible, through aggregation, to eliminate a redundant equation in models that *assume* the system is over-determined.

There is no mystery about this. It is well known that by virtue of the simultaneity assumption implicit in the Walrasian budget constraint *a causal analysis of dynamic behavior is impossible in Walrasian models*. It is the mythical Walrasian *tâtonnement/* recontract auctioneer that *causes* prices to change within the Walrasian paradigm, not decision-making units that actually exist in the real world.

This does not mean models that rely on this methodology are not useful or meaningful. They are, in fact, exceedingly useful and have proven to be invaluable in the analysis of economic problems. But it does mean that such models cannot be used to establish the temporal order in which events must occur—that is, the order in which their endogenous variables must change in response to a change in an exogenous variable—and, thus, *they cannot provide the basis for a causal analysis of dynamic behavior.*

The reason Marshall is *essential* to understanding causality in Keynes' general theory (and in economics in general for that matter) can be seen by examining the role played by the *ceteris paribus* assumption of this paradigm in the simple dynamics of supply and demand within the context of a Marshallian partial equilibrium analysis. This kind of analysis is generally explained in terms of a competitive market characterized by an upward sloping supply curve and a downward sloping demand curve as shown in **Figure 1**, a diagram that any student who has taken a principles course in economics should recognize immediately and understand implicitly. This figure illustrates a situation in which a market begins with an equilibrium price **P** and quantity **Q** as determined by the intersection of the initial supply curve **S** (which shows the quantities suppliers are *willing* to sell at various prices) and demand curve **D** (which shows the quantities demanders are *willing* to purchase at various prices) and then experiences a *ceteris paribus* increase in supply that shifts the supply curve from **S** to **S\***:

**Figure 1: Simple Dynamics of Supply and Demand.**

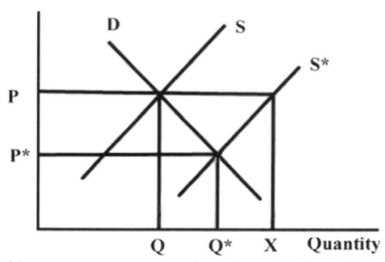

This creates an excess supply at the original equilibrium price equal to the difference between **Q** and **X** which is the quantity in excess of the amount suppliers are *willing* to sell over the amount buyers are *willing* to buy at the original equilibrium price **P**.

Since we are assuming a competitive market we can expect suppliers to attempt to increase their output at the original price **P** and that competition among suppliers and demanders will *cause* the market price to fall and *cause* the quantity produced for, and sold in the market to increase until the new partial equilibrium price **P**\* and quantity **Q**\* are achieved at the intersection of the initial demand curve **D** and the new supply curve **S**\*. At this price and quantity, and only at this price and quantity, it will be possible for suppliers to sell all they are *willing* to sell and demanders to purchase all they are *willing* to purchase, and there is no reason for demanders or suppliers to change the price or quantity produced and exchanged in the market in this *ceteris paribus* situation.

The significance of this kind of analysis is not simply that it makes it possible to predict how a *ceteris paribus* change in supply or demand will affect the partial-equilibrium value of price and quantity in an isolated market. Its significance lies in the fact that it provides an *analytic framework* within which it is possible to identify and to isolate those factors—including *the non-price factors* that affect the willingness to buy and sell that determine the *positions* of the supply and demand curves—that *in themselves* have a *direct* effect on the determination of the quantity produced for, and traded in a given market and the price at which exchange takes place in the market. This, in turn, makes it possible to examine systematically the *causal interactions* between markets in terms of the effects of a change in a determinant of either supply or demand in a given market on the price and quantity produced and exchanged in that market *over time* beginning with an examination of the way in which price and quantities are affected in that market. It is then possible to consider the effects of changes in the price and quantity exchanged in the given market on the behavior of participants in other markets (substitutes and compliments) and the feedback effects in the given market of the changes in prices and quantities exchanged in other markets, *ad infinitum* if one wishes until a partial or general equilibrium is achieved.[23]

This example of the simple dynamics of supply and demand assumes a competitive market, but even if the market is not competitive we can still use Marshall's *ceteris paribus* methodology to examine the *cause* and *effect* implications of various kinds of non-competitive phenomena with which we are confronted as anyone who has taken an undergraduate intermediate microeconomics course or read Marshall's *Principles* well knows.[24]  And even when the assumptions underlying the analysis are not fully met, the overall contribution of the metaphorical application of this kind of analysis to the understanding of practical economic problems is such that it is an indispensable part of the economist's way of thinking.  One might even say: "This is the nature of economic thinking." In any event, this was clearly the nature of Keynes' thinking as he wrote *The General Theory*:

> The object of our analysis is, not to provide a machine, or method of blind manipulation, which will furnish an infallible answer, but to provide ourselves with an organized and orderly method of thinking out particular problems; and, after we have reached a provisional

---

[23] This is, of course, a very simplistic discussion of the nature of Marshall's method of analysis, the kind of discussion given in an undergraduate textbook. To fully appreciate the brilliance of Marshall's methodology it is necessary to actually read Marshall, and it must be emphasized at this point that the feedback effects that are assumed to take place as markets interact within the Marshallian paradigm are assumed to take place *through time*. Cf., Kwak

[24] See, for example, Crotty (2002).

conclusion by isolating the complicating factors one by one, we then have to go back on ourselves and allow, as well as we can, for the probable interactions of the factors amongst themselves. This is the nature of economic thinking. *Any other way of applying our formal principles of thought (without which, however, we shall be lost in the wood) will lead us into error.* It is a great fault of symbolic pseudo-mathematical methods of formalizing a system of economic analysis...that *they expressly assume strict independence between the factors involved* and lose all their cogency and authority if this hypothesis is disallowed; whereas, in ordinary discourse, where we are not blindly manipulating but know all the time what we are doing and what the words mean, we can keep 'at the back of our heads' the necessary reserves and qualifications and the adjustments which we shall have to make later on, *in a way in which we cannot keep complicated partial differentials 'at the back' of several pages of algebra which assume that they all vanish.* Too large a proportion of recent 'mathematical' economics are merely concoctions, as imprecise as the initial assumptions they rest on, which allow the author to lose sight of the complexities and interdependencies of the real world in a maze of pretentious and unhelpful symbols. (Keynes, 1936, [*emphasis* added] pp. 297-8)

This is the methodology of Marshall, not of Walras, and the *methodology* described in this passage and embodied in the simple example presented in **Figure 1** is the single most powerful analytical tool available to economists as a guide to understanding how the economic system actually works in the real world. There are two reasons for this:

1.  The *ceteris paribus* assumption of the Marshallian paradigm makes it possible to *explain* the determination of prices and quantities and what will

*cause* prices and quantities to *change* in terms of the behavior of those decision-making units (i.e., buyers and sellers in the simple example above) that actually have the *power* to determine and change prices and quantities bought and sold in markets.

2.  There must be a change in the variables that affect the behavior of those decision-making units that actually have the power to determine and change prices and quantities bought and sold in markets (i.e., supply or demand must change) *before* a change in price or quantity can occur within the Marshallian paradigm.  This makes it possible to establish *the temporal order in which events must occur* which makes it possible to separate *cause* and *effect*.

It is these two characteristics of Marshall's *ceteris paribus* methodology that make it possible to provide a *causal explanation of dynamic behavior* within the context of the Marshallian paradigm, and this is why the seminal issue with regard to the theory of interest raised by Keynes in *The General Theory* is whether or not the loanable-funds theory is consistent with the Marshallian paradigm of supply and demand.[25]

That the loanable-funds theory is not consistent with the Marshallian paradigm and that the liquidity-preference theory is, in fact, *implied* by this paradigm can be seen by comparing the two theories within the

---

[25]It must be noted that Marshall's supply and demand methodology is also the single most powerful analytical tool available to *misrepresent* how the economic system works by those who use this tool in a fallacious manner. See blackford (2020, ch. 6) Friedman (1949), Kwak, Kuttner, Madrick, Smith, Schlefer, and section **II-c** below.

context of this paradigm in light of Keynes' objection to the loanable-funds theory.

## II-b. Loanable Funds and Marshall

In writing *A Treatise on Money*, Keynes discovered it is not enough to know what is happening to the *flows* of saving and investment to know what is happening to the prices of assets. He also had to know what is happening to output and the supply and demand for the *stock* of money. The fact that *money or debt (i.e., borrowed money) is required as a medium of exchange in a monetary economy* implies that, given output and the supply and demand for money, changes in the amount saved by savers in response to an increase in saving must be exactly offset by changes in the total value of assets *willingly* relinquished by investors. As a result, there is no way to explain *why* savers or investors would be *willing* to change the prices of assets in response to a change in either saving or investment if output and the supply and demand for money remained unchanged.

This is the essence of Keynes' old argument in *A Treatise on Money* quoted at length in section **I-a** above, and what this means is that, given the *ceteris paribus* assumptions on which this argument is based, Keynes could not use the Marshallian paradigm of supply and demand to explain the determination of the prices of assets if he were to assume that the prices of assets are determined by savers and investors.

Within the analytic framework developed by Keynes throughout *The General Theory*, this argument translates into the argument that, if the *flow* of income and the supply and demand for *stock* of money are assumed to be given, the Marshallian paradigm of supply and demand cannot be used to explain the way in which rates of interest (or prices of assets) are determined if it is assumed that rates of interest (or prices of assets) are determined by the *flow* of saving and investment.  Nor can they be explained by the supply and demand for loanable funds if the supply and demand for loanable funds are defined in terms of the *flow* of saving and investment.

If we think of *the rate of interest* in terms of "the complex of the various rates of interest current for different periods of time, i.e. for debts of different maturities" (Keynes, 1936, p. 167n) "and risks" (p. 28),[26] the inconsistency of the loanable-funds theory with the Marshallian paradigm of supply and demand implicit in Keynes' old argument can be explained by way of **Figure 2** below which illustrates the direct effects of a *ceteris paribus* increase in the propensity to save on the rate of interest within the Marshallian paradigm.  In this figure, **S** represents the initial position of the *flow* of loanable-funds supply curve as determined by saving, and **D** represents the initial position of the *flow* of loanable-funds demand curve as determined by investment; **R** and **L** denote the initial market and equilibrium rate of interest (as defined above) and the *flow* of loanable funds, respectively.

If it is assumed that a *ceteris paribus* increase in saving increases the supply of loanable funds by shifting **S** to **S\*** in **Figure 2** and leaves the demand for loanable funds unchanged at **D**, the new equilibrium rate of interest and flow of loanable funds predicted by these curves are given by **R\*** and **L\*** at the intersec-

---

[26] Cf., Fisher (1930, pp. 34-5).

tion of the initial loanable-funds demand curve **D** and the new loanable funds supply curve **S***.  This will create a *theoretical* excess supply of loanable funds at the initial rate of interest **R** equal to the difference between **X** and **L**.  But even though the new equilibrium rate of interest is predicted to be at **R***, it cannot be assumed suppliers and demanders of loanable funds will react to this excess supply at the initial rate of interest **R** in such a way as to drive the market rate of interest to **R***:

**Figure 2:  Loanable Funds and Marshall.**

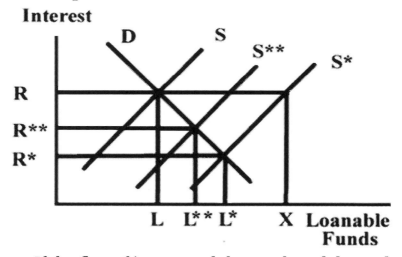

If the *flow* of income and the supply and demand for the *stock* of money are to remain unchanged in this *ceteris paribus* situation, producers of consumption goods will no longer be able to replenish the transactions and precautionary balances needed to maintain their scale of operations through sales.  As a result, in order to maintain their scale of operations they must be willing to either borrow *money* or sell assets to obtain the *money* needed to maintain these balances as the demand for consumption goods falls.

By way of Keynes' old argument, this means that the producers of consumption goods must be willing to increase borrowing or decrease their stocks of assets *at the same rate* savers are willing to increase lending and increase their stocks of assets if the level of output and the supply and demand for money are to remain unchanged.

As a result, savers will be able to lend all of the money they are willing to lend at the initial rate of interest and purchase all of the assets they are willing to purchase at the initial prices of assets, and investors will be able to borrow all of the money they are willing to borrow at the initial rate of interest and sell all of the assets they are willing to sell at the initial prices of assets. So long as the initial *flow* of income and supply and demand for the *stock* of money are maintained in this situation, there is no way in which investors can force savers to accept lower rates of interest or higher prices of assets, and there is no way in which savers can force investors to accept higher rates of interest or lower prices of assets. Thus, there is no economic reason for the market rate of interest to fall in the *ceteris paribus* situation illustrated in **Figure 2** since *there exist no market forces that can cause either rates of interest or prices of assets to change* other than through portfolio-balance effects which can go either way.[27]

---

[27] If the increase in saving takes the form of an increase in the demand for government bonds or corporate debt, and producers attempt to sustain their operations through an increase in the demand for trade credit or bank loans we would expect a decrease in the former rates of interest and an offsetting increase in the latter. If the increase in saving takes the form of an increase in the demand for non-debt assets and producers increase borrowing we would expect an *increase* in rates of in-

In addition, even if employment, output, and income fall, as both Robertson and Keynes argued they must fall in this situation, there is still no reason to believe this will cause the market rate of interest to fall to **R***.  Since income is one of the non-price factors that affect the willingness to lend that are subsumed in the functional form of the loanable-funds supply curve, *a change in income must cause a shift in the loanable-funds supply curve and, thereby, change the equilibrium rate of interest given by the intersection of the loanable-funds supply and demand curves.*

If, for example, there is a fall in income that causes the loanable-funds supply curve to fall from **S*** to

---

terest and prices of non-debt assets since there would be no increase in the willingness to lend or to sell non-debt assets to offset the increase in the willingness to borrow and to buy non-debt assets. For the same reason, we would also expect an *increase* in the rate of interest if producers borrow and the increase in saving takes the form of an increase in the demands for precautionary or speculative balances. Only if savers buy *bonds* and producers sell *non-debt assets* or run down their holding of precautionary or speculative balances (*to the extent this is possible*) would we expect the rate of interest to decrease in this *ceteris paribus* situation.

It is important to note, however, that these are portfolio balance decisions that involve changes in the supplies and demands for money and non-debt assets, not saving and investment decisions. Since a) there is no *a priori* reason to believe that changes in saving or investment determine the nature of the incompatibility, b) the changes in the rate of interest and price of non-debt assets can go either way depending on the nature of the incompatibility, and c) these kinds of changes in the rate of interest and price of non-debt assets occur even when there is no change in saving or investment these changes cannot be explained in terms of changes in saving or investment; they must be explained in terms of changes in the supplies and demands for money and non-debt assets.  See Keynes (1930, pp. 130-1; 1936, p. 186n), Bibow (2000a; 2001; 2009, Sec. 3.4).

**S\*\*** in **Figure 2** the equilibrium rate of interest that is supposedly given by the intersection of the new loanable-funds supply curve **S\*\*** and the initial loanable-funds demand curve **D** must increase to **R\*\*** away from **R\*** and back toward the initial rate or interest **R**. There is obviously no reason to expect the market rate of interest to fall to **R\*** in this situation, *nor is there any reason to expect the market rate of interest to fall to the new theoretical equilibrium rate ostensibly given by R\*\**.

As employment and output fall in the consumption-goods industries, the need to borrow money and sell assets to maintain transactions and precautionary balances at the initial rate of interest **R** must also fall. At the same time, *the fall in income must cause saving to fall at the initial rate of interest R by exactly the same amount as the need to borrow money and sell assets falls.* Why should we expect the rate of interest to change as saving, and, therefore, the amount of loanable-funds supplied falls by exactly the same amount as the need to borrow money and sell assets and, therefore, the willingness to borrow falls?

There is no reason to expect anything about *changes* in the market rate of interest with regard to the intersection of these two curves since, *by virtue of Keynes' old argument,* these two curves tell us nothing at all about the actual behavior of suppliers and demanders in the loanable funds market in response to a change in either saving or investment *in the absence of an explanation of what is happening to the supply and demand for money.*

Robertson imagined a smooth transfer of resources out of the consumption-goods industries into the investment-goods industries that will drive the market rate of interest to **R\*** in **Figure 2** as the system adjusts to an increase in saving, barring "the existence of [a] siding or trap" caused by a negative interest rate sensitivity of the demand for money. If there is a negative interest rate sensitivity of the demand for money Robertson assumed the rate of interest will come to rest at some point such as **R\*\*** at a rate of interest higher than **R\*** but less than **R**. The only way to make sense out of this argument is if we assume the system *somehow* adjusts from **R** to **R\*** with no change in income such that **S\*** does not change, or if income does change and **S\*** shifts to **S\*\*** we *somehow* end up at **R\*\***.[28] This may make sense as a *description* of the change in the short-run *static-equilibrium* rate of interest without or with a negative interest rate sensitivity of the demand for money, given the assumptions, whatever these assumptions may be, on which these equilibrium positions are assumed to depend, but, this tells us nothing about how these equilibriums are obtained.

As we have seen, if income does not change in this *ceteris paribus* situation there is no reason to believe the rate of interest will change, and even if income does change we still have no reason to believe the rate of interest will change *based on the information contained in Figure 2*. Clearly, **Figure 2** tells us nothing at all about the market rate of interest *as it changes* from one point of static equilibrium to another whether **R\*** or **R\*\*** is the new point of short-run equilibrium or not. *It is simply impossible to give a logically consistent, causal explanation of the dynamic behavior* of *the rate of interest based on the infor-*

---

[28] Cf., Robertson (1940, pp. 18-9) quoted at length in section **I-d** above.

*mation contained in* **Figure 2**.[29]

The fundamental contradiction in the loanable-funds theory with the Marshallian paradigm that we see in trying to analyze the *dynamic* behavior of the rate of interest in **Figure 2** arises from the very nature of the circular flow of the *stock* of money in sustaining the *flows* of income, credit, and expenditures in a *monetary economy*. Whenever decision-making units are unable to obtain the *money* needed to finance their desired transactions otherwise, they have no place to turn if they are to execute those transactions *in a monetary economy* except to the credit market or to the markets for assets in order to obtain the *money* needed to finance those transactions. As a result, prices of assets and rates of interest on loans and debts cannot change in response to a *ceteris paribus* increase in saving if income and the supply and demand for money are given even if the increase in saving takes "the form of an increased demand for securities."

All that is necessary to understand what this means with regard to Keynes' general theory is to follow the *causal chain of events* implied by Marshall's *ceteris paribus* methodology as the system adjusts to the increase in saving examined in **Figure 2**. What is significant about the *ceteris paribus* increase in saving examined in **Figure 2** is that while there are no economic reasons for rates of interest or prices of assets to change in this situation, *there are economic reasons for employment, output, and income to change*. The accumulation of debt and depletion of

---

[29] See Bibow (2000a; 2001).

marketable assets on the part of producers of consumption goods must eventually lead to a change in *expectations* with regard to the *profitability* of continuing to maintain their current scale of operations. This change in *expectations* must motivate producers in the consumption-goods industries to reduce employment and output. The resulting fall in *income* can be expected to continue until the willingness to save is equal to the willingness to invest since it is at this point, and only at this point, that producers in the consumption-goods industries will be able to eliminate the necessity to increase debt or sell assets in order obtain the *money* needed to maintain their scale of operations.

This means that in order to provide *a logically consistent, causal explanation* of the way in which a change in saving or investment affects the economic system *through time* that is consistent with Marshall's *ceteris paribus* methodology it must be assumed that income*, not the rate of interest,* is determined by saving and investment since it is the equilibrium level of income, not the equilibrium rate of interest, that is determined by saving and investment, and there are market forces that *ceteris paribus* can be expected to move the level income to this equilibrium.

Furthermore, the fall in income that results from a change in expectations in response to an increase in saving must, in turn, cause a fall in the demand for money. *And just as there are economic reasons for income to change in response to a ceteris paribus change in saving, there are economic reasons for the rate of interest to change in response to a ceteris paribus fall in the demand for money.*

Given the supply of money, a *ceteris paribus* fall

in income must cause a fall in the demands for transactions and precautionary balances that increases the *supply* of speculative balances, that is—*money balances decision-making units have no use for other than to lend or to hold as an asset.*[30]   What happens to the prices of non-debt assets in this situation will depend on the supplies and demands for non-debt assets, *but what happens to the rate of interest will depend crucially on what happens to the supply and demand for money.*[31]   To the extent the increase in the supply of speculative balances increases the willingness of wealth holders to purchase new and existing debt, competition for new and existing debt must, *ceteris paribus,* lead to a decrease in the rate of interest.   As the resulting decrease in the rate of interest increases the capitalized value of existing non-debt assets and, thereby, lowers the prospective rates of return on non-debt assets (Fisher, 1930, pp. 14-29) it must force members of the nonbank public (i.e., wealth holders) to either a) accumulate money balances for which they have no use other than to hold as an asset or b) accept lower rates of interest on the debt assets they choose to accumulate.   At the same time, banks will be forced to either a) accumulate reserves relative to their other assets or b) accept lower rates of interest on the debt assets they choose to ac-

---

[30]See Keynes (1936, p. 171). The mechanisms by which the supply of speculative balances is determined are examined in detail in the formal model specified in Blackford (2020, ch. 5). The transactions demand for money is assumed to include both real and non-debt financial transactions in this model since, as is explained in Blackford (2020, ch. 4), balances held for the purposes of purchasing assets must be included in the demand for money.

[31] The way in which the prices of non-debt assets are determined is examined in Blackford (2020, ch. 6).

cumulate.

Keynes argued (1936, ch. 13) that as rates of interest fall below the rates wealth-holders *expect* to be realized in the future, wealth holders will be motivated to hold a larger portion of their wealth in the form of money (i.e., highly liquid resources) and a smaller portion in the form of debt in an attempt to minimize the risk of a capital loss on holdings of debt in the future. (Keynes, 1936, Chs 13-17) Thus, to the extent the resulting fall in rates of interest enhances the willingness of wealth holders to hold their wealth in the form of money, that is—*to willingly accumulate speculative balances to hold as an asset*—the quantity of money demanded must increase. And to the extent the resulting fall in rates of interest enhances the willingness of banks to accumulate reserves the quantity of money supplied must fall. The fall in rates of interest can be expected to continue, *ceteris paribus*, in this situation until the quantity of money supplied is equal to the quantity of money demanded for it is at this point, and only at this point, that rates of interest will equalize the marginal advantage of wealth holders holding speculative balances as an asset or holding debt, and the marginal advantage of banks holding reserves or holding debt, and there is no economic reason for rates of interest or the *stock* of money to change.[32]

---

[32] Keynes generally assumed the supply of money to be exogenously determined by the monetary authorities in *The General Theory*, but in December of 1937 he noted that:

> Dr. Herbert Bab has suggested to me that one could regard the rate of interest as being determined by the interplay of the terms on which the public desires to become more or less liquid and those on which the banking system is ready to become more or less un-

What this means is that in order to provide *a logically consistent, causal explanation* of the way in which a change in savings or investment affects the economic system *through time* that is consistent with Marshall's *ceteris paribus* methodology it not only must be assumed that income, not the rate of interest, is determined by savings and investment, *it must also be assumed that the rate of interest, not income, is determined by the supply and demand for money* since it is the equilibrium rate of interest, not the equilibrium level of income, that is determined by the supply and demand for money, and there are market forces that *ceteris paribus* can be expected to move the rate of interest to this equilibrium.[33]

---

liquid. This is, I think, an illuminating way of expressing the liquidity-theory of the rate of interest; but particularly so within the field of 'finance.' (Dec. 1937, p.666),

See also Keynes (1936, chs. 13, 15, and 17; June 1937, p.241; Dec. 1937, p.668; June, 1938, p. 319) and Blackford (2020, ch. 5). The supply of money is considered to be endogenous in the text above, but it can be assumed to be exogenous if one wishes. It should also be noted that Bibow (2005) examines the way in which Keynes' liquidity preference theory can be related to the portfolio choices of banks.

[33] See Keynes (1936, p. 186n) quoted at the beginning of this chapter. Keynes noted that the distinction between debt and non-debt assets in *The General Theory* removes the "confusion [in the *Treatise*] between results due to a change in the rate of interest and those due to a change in the schedule of the marginal efficiency of capital," (pp. 173-4) and he drew a clear distinction between the way in which changes in the prospective yield on non-debt assets and changes in the rate of interest affect the demand for money:

It might be thought that, in the same way, an individual, who believed that the prospective yield of investments will be below what the market is expecting, will have a sufficient reason for holding liquid cash. But this is not the case. He has a sufficient reason for holding cash or debts in preference to equities; but the purchase of debts will be a preferable alternative to holding cash, unless he also

This also means that Robertson's view of causality can find no theoretical justification within the Marshallian paradigm of supply and demand. Robertson's *ad hoc* assertion that an increase in saving "lowers the rate of interest quite directly through swelling the money stream of demand for securities; and that this fall in the rate of interest increases the proportion of resources over which people wish to keep command in monetary form" (1940, pp. 18-9) has it backwards. Arguing that an increase in thriftiness "lowers the rate of interest quite directly" implies that the rate of interest can fall *before* there is a decrease in income and an increase in the supply of speculative balances in this situation. This runs afoul of what may be called the *ante hoc, ergo propter hoc* fallacy. Such arguments only make sense to those who believe an *effect* (i.e., the fall in the rate of interest) can come *before* its *cause* (i.e., the increase in the *supply* of speculative balances), which is apparently what Johnson believed when he wrote:

> In a dynamic context, the loanable-funds theory definitely makes more economic sense; and the sustained

---

believes that the future rate of interest will prove to be higher than the market is supposing. (1936, p. 170n)

It should also be noted that while it might be thought an individual who believed the future rate of interest will be above what the market is expecting will have a sufficient reason to hold non-debt assets in preference to liquid cash, but since the "derivation of the value of every durable agent or good involves the discounting or capitalizing of income," (Fisher, 1930, p. 42) an expectation of an increasing rate of interest in the future is also an expectation of decreasing prices of non-debt assets in the future. Thus, holding money will be preferable to purchasing non-debt assets in this situation unless the individual also believes the prospective yields on non-debt assets "will prove to be higher than the market is supposing." See Keynes (Feb. 1939).

resistance of Keynesians to admitting it, evident most notably in the prolonged defense...of the proposition that an increase in the propensity to save lowers the interest rate only by reducing the level of income, is a credit to their ingenuity rather than their scientific spirit. (1961, pp. 6-7)

The "ingenuity" that Johnson complained about in this passage was on the part of those who accepted the basic principles of supply and demand in defiance of the "scientific spirit" of those who insisted that within "a dynamic context, the loanable-funds theory definitely makes more economic sense" by way of an *ante hoc, ergo propter hoc* argument that begins with the assumption that an increase in the propensity to save "lowers the rate of interest quite directly" and then attempted to rationalize this assertion by arguing that the choices of decision-making units are constrained by sales. As we saw in **Chapter I**, this rationalization only makes sense in a *static* analysis which assumes expectations are unit-elastic and adjust instantaneously to changes in sales—an assumption that ignores the temporal order in which events must occur, and, in so doing, *renders a causal analysis of dynamic behavior meaningless.*

Given the supply of money the rate of interest cannot change in response to a *ceteris paribus* increase in saving until *after* there has been:

1. a change in expectations that

2. leads to a fall in employment, output, and income that

3. decreases the demand for transactions and precautionary balances that

4. increases the supply of speculative balances that

5.  forces wealth holders to choose between increasing their holdings of money as an asset or debt and banks to choose between increasing their holdings of reserves or debt.

This causal chain of events must occur before the rate of interest can fall in response to a *ceteris paribus* increase in saving in a monetary economy, that is—in an economy in which either money or debt (i.e., borrowed money) is required as a medium of exchange. The direction of causality runs from changes in saving and investment, to changes in income, to changes in the demand for money, to changes in the rate of interest. In light of Keynes' old argument, it defies the laws of supply and demand (not to mention the laws of logic and reason) to argue that causality runs in the opposite direction from changes in the rate of interest to changes in the quantity of speculative balances demanded before there is an increase the supply of speculative balances brought about by a fall in the demand for transactions balances.[34]

What this means is that it is impossible to provide a *logically consistent, causal explanation* of the way in which a *change* in saving or investment affects the economic system *through time* that does not fall prey to Robertson's *ante hoc, ergo propter hoc* fallacy if it is assumed that the rate of interest is determined by saving and investment. Nor is it possible to provide a *logically consistent, causal* explanation of the way in which a *change* in saving or investment affects the economic system *through time* if the rate of interest is assumed to be determined by the supply and demand

---

[34] See Bibow (2000a; 2001).

for loanable funds if the supply and demand for loanable funds are defined in terms of the *flows* of saving and investment.

## II-c. Liquidity Preference and Marshall

That Keynes' liquidity-preference theory is fundamentally different than the above can be seen by examining the effects on the rate of interest of a *ceteris paribus* increase in thriftiness that takes the form of an increase in the demand for securities within the context of Keynes' liquidity-preference theory.  This situation is illustrated in **Figure 3** where **S** represents the initial position of the money supply curve and **D** the initial position of the money demand curve; **R** and **M** denote the initial market and equilibrium rate of interest and stock of money, respectively.

Since an increase in thriftiness that takes the form of an increase in the demand for securities cannot have a *direct* effect on the demand or supply of money in the liquidity-preference theory other than by way of portfolio-balance effects which can go either way, there is no reason to assume the rate of interest will either increase or decrease as a direct result of the increase in thriftiness.  It can, however, have an *indirect* effect on the rate of interest through its effects on expectations and income.

To the extent an increase in thriftiness leads to a subsequent change in expectations that, in turn, causes a *ceteris paribus* fall in employment, output, and income, the demand for money must fall.  This situation is represented in **Figure 3** by the shift in the demand for money curve from **D** to **D\***:

Figure 3: Liquidity Preference and Marshall.

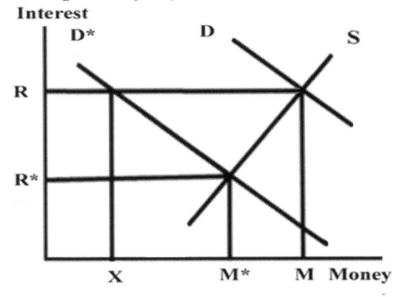

This fall in the demand for money must cause the theoretical equilibrium rate of interest and stock of money to fall from **R** and **M** to **R\*** and **M\***. The result is an excess supply of money at the initial rate of interest **R** equal to the difference between **M** and **X**, and, unlike the loanable-funds theory, there are market forces that will cause the market rate of interest to fall to **R\*** in this *ceteris paribus* situation.

As we have seen, the fall in income will reduce the demand for transactions and precautionary balances and, therefore, the willingness of decision-making units to secure or maintain these balances. Given the supply of money, this must increase the supply of speculative balances. As speculative balances accumulate, competition for new loans and existing debt must *cause* the rate of interest to fall until the stock of money supplied is equal to the stock of money demanded, for it is at this point **M\***, and only at this point, that the rate of interest **R\*** equalizes the marginal advantages of wealth holders holding money/debt and banks holding reserves/debt, and there is no way for wealth holders to achieve a higher rate of interest and no reason for banks to accept a lower rate of interest.[35]

Thus, as falling income decreases the demand for money there are market forces to drive the market rate of interest, *ceteris paribus*, from **R** to **R\*** in **Figure 3**, and it is possible to provide a *logically consistent, causal explanation* of the *dynamic behavior* of the rate of interest as it adjusts to this new point of equilibrium within the context of Keynes' liquidity-preference theory by way of the supply and demand for money curves in **Figure 3**.

What is most important to observe about this example, however, is:

1.  The forces that are assumed to drive the market

---

[35] It is perhaps worth noting at this point that, "in general, a *change* in expectations…will only produce its full effect on employment over a considerable period," (Keynes, 1936, p. 47) and even after producers are no longer willing to maintain the scale of production in this situation they may still be forced to sell assets and borrow money in order to satisfy the transaction demand for money needed to meet the contractual obligations they committed to leading up to the fall in the demand for consumption goods—obligations that can no longer be financed through sales or precautionary balances.  There may also be a need for alternative financing of transactions balances that result from what Marshall referred to as an attempt to not "spoil markets." (pp. 218-20)

It should also be noted that the transactions demand for money can become rather intense when it comes to the willingness to borrow money to obtain these balances given the fact that firms forego acquiring these balances at the cost of forgoing investment opportunities as well as at the risk of defaulting on contractual obligation, and households forego acquiring these balances at the cost of forgone consumption and at the risk of defaulting on contractual obligations as well.

rate of interest from **R** to **R\*** in **Figure 3** can be explained in terms of the choices of those decision-making units that actually have the *power* to affect changes in the rate of interest, that is—*demanders and suppliers of money*—as the existence of surpluses and shortages in the *stock* of *money* affect their willingness and ability to borrow and lend *money*.

2.  As the effects of an increase in the propensity to save work their way through the system, there is nothing to prevent demanders and suppliers of money from continuing to adjust the rate of interest *toward* the rate of interest that equates the supply and demand for money *at each point in time* as the system adjusts *through time* whether the rest of the system is in equilibrium or not.

3.  There is no reason to assume the new state of equilibrium that results from an increase in thriftiness will leave income unchanged.

   Robertson apparently recognized this last point in the passage quoted in section **I-d** above where he notes that an interest rate sensitivity of the demand for money could lead to "there being a net decline in total money income, i.e. of money incomes not expanding in one sector to the extent that they are contracting in the other." But if income changes in this situation we cannot know the position of the new short-run equilibrium supply of loanable-funds curve **S\*\*** in **Figure 2** without first knowing the level of income that equates the willingness to save and invest. Thus, we cannot know the new short-run equilibrium value of the rate of interest **R\*\*** based on the information contained in **Figure 2**. **Figure 2** can only tell us that the new equilibrium rate of interest will be **R\*** if income and, therefore, the supply of loanable funds do not change.

Robertson and his fellow anti-Keynesians dealt with this problem by assuming the equilibrium values of income and the rate of interest are determined simultaneously within each period. What they missed is that by denying the relevance of Keynes' old argument to their intraperiod dynamic analysis as to how this equilibrium comes about they limited the relevance of their intraperiod dynamic arguments to the imaginary world of the Walrasian auctioneer.

The same approach was adopted by the Keynesians as they followed Robertson's lead when they chose to adopt Hicks' IS/LM model which combines the supply and demand for money with saving and investment to arrive at the equilibrium rate of interest and level of income simultaneously. This simply begged the question of *causality* raised by Keynes since the Keynesians' method of approach was Walrasian and, therefore, descriptive and static. Even though some Keynesians defended the logic of Keynes' old argument in their debate with the anti-Keynesians, the vast majority failed to grasp the relevance of this logic to Keynes' causal/dynamic methodology and what this logic means with regard to the *irrelevance* of Walras' Law and the Walrasian auctioneer to the way in which the rate of interest is determined in Keynes' general theory. As a result, when the Keynesians adopted Hicks' IS/LM model they did not adopt Keynes' causal/dynamic methodology in spite of the fact that *there was nothing to prevent them from doing so* other than their fidelity to the *tâtonnement/* recontract methodology of Walras and their inability to grasp or to appreciate the fact that Marshall's caus-al/dynamic methodology is the *sine qua non* of cau-sality in Keynes' general theory and in economics in general.[36]

The position of the Keynesians in this regard was best summarized by Lawrence R. Klein in 1966:

> Keynes took income to be the important variable in the savings investment equation, and took interest to be the important variable in the liquidity-preference equation. In the end result of the most general Keynesian system one cannot pick out cause and effect. The interest theo-ry of this system is the solution to the entire set of equations *which is based on the liquidity-preference building block*. (p. 97)

This completely misses the point of Keynes' li-quidity-preference theory, namely, that Keynes' theo-ry makes possible what is impossible in the classical theory. Once it is realized that

1.     rates of interest and the prices of *stocks* of as-sets are determined by the supplies and de-mands for *stocks* of assets—including the *stock* of money—in the markets for assets, and

2.     the prices and quantities of *flows* of economic goods and resources are determined by the supplies and demands for the *flows* of econom-ic goods and resources in the markets for eco-nomic goods and resources,

it then becomes possible to establish the causal inter-actions within and between these two kinds of mar-kets by way of the Marshallian paradigm.

---

[36] Cf. Bibow (2001).

Keynes' Marshallian approach to the theories of consumption, investment, interest, and money, when combined with his understanding of the way in which expectations affect economic behavior, provides an analytic framework in which the interactions within and between these fundamentally different kinds of markets can be analyzed, understood, and explained within the context of a single, integrated paradigm in which a logically consistent, causal analysis of dynamic behavior is possible.   This is the very essence of Keynes' general theory.[37]

## II-d. Ohlin's Ex-Ante/Ex-Post Distraction

At this point it should be clear that Ohlin was mistaken in his belief that to reject the loanable-funds

---

[37] Keynes observed that:

> The psychological time-preferences of an individual require two distinct sets of decisions….The first is concerned with that aspect of time-preference which I have called the *propensity to consume*, which…determines for each individual how much of his income he will consume and how much he will reserve in *some* form of command over future consumption.

> But this decision having been made, there is a further decision which awaits him, namely, in *what form* he will hold the command over future consumption which he has reserved, whether out of his current income or from previous savings. (Keynes, 1936, p. 166)

These are two fundamentally different kinds of decisions that relate to two fundamentally different kinds of markets: The first is an income statement decision that relates to markets for *flows* of goods and resources.   The second is a balance sheet decision that relates to markets for *stocks* of assets.   The only way to understand the interactions within and between these phenomena is through a system of double entry book-keeping of the kind implicit in Keynes' theories of consumption, investment, interest, and money that clearly distinguishes between these two kinds of decisions.   See Blackford (2020, ch. 6) for a discussion of the neoclassical approach to this problem as opposed to Keynes' approach, and cf., Bibow (2009), Lavoie and Godley, Klein (1966, pp. 123), and De Scitovszky.

theory one must "refute also the Marshallian supply and demand curve analysis *in toto*." In fact, the converse is true; to accept Ohlin's arguments one must refute the Marshallian supply and demand curve analysis *in toto*. The loanable-funds theory can neither predict the effect of a *ceteris paribus* change in the market rate of interest nor can it provide a causal explanation of the way in which the market rate of interest is determined. It is clearly inconsistent with the Marshallian paradigm. There is simply no way to salvage the loanable-funds theory along the lines Ohlin was attempting to salvage it through distinguishing between *ex ante* plans and *ex post* results if we accept Marshall's supply and demand curve interpretation of these concepts.

The nature of the problem can be seen by considering a situation in which there is an increase in the propensity to save and, hence, by definition, a fall in the propensity to consume that arises as a result of, say, a national tragedy such as 9/11. People feel insecure, and in response they consume less and allow a larger portion of their incomes to accumulate in their bank accounts than they otherwise would. How will this increase in the propensity to save, accompanied by an increase in the accumulation of money balances by households, affect the rate of interest in a *ceteris paribus* situation in which the supply of money and income do not change?

Within the context of Keynes' liquidity-preference theory, the accumulation of these balances would be seen as an increase in the precautionary demand for money on the part of households. As these balances accumulate the reduction in the demand for consumption goods reduces the flow of money to firms in the consumption-goods industries.  In the absence of a change in income there would be no decrease in the demand for transactions or precautionary balances on the part of firms, and firms would find they could no longer replenish these balances from sales as these balances are expended over time.  In order to obtain the *money* needed to meet their expenditure obligations firms would be forced to either increase borrowing or sell assets to obtain the needed funds.  As the demand for money on the part of households increases with no change in the demand for money on the part of firms the net effect would be an increase in the total demand for money.  Thus, in the absence of an increase in the supply of money, we would expect the increase in the demand for precautionary balances to create an excess demand for money at the existing rate of interest and competition among demanders and suppliers of money to cause an *increase* in the rate of interest in order to induce banks to increase the quantity of money supplied and wealth holders to reduce their demands for speculative and investment finance balances to make these balances available to households and firms to meet their transactions and precautionary needs.[38]

How can this situation be explained within the loanable-funds theory?  The only way it would seem to make sense is if we were to assume the increase in the propensity to save that made it impossible for businesses to replenish their transactions and precautionary balances through sales and forced firms to increase their borrowing *caused* an increase in the loan-

---

[38] See the formal model specified in Blackford (2020, ch. 5) for an explanation as to how investment finance balances enter this scenario.

able-funds demand curve. The problem is, once this assumption is made the supply and demand for loanable funds become *ex-post* functions that are useless for analytical purposes. The rate of interest at which these two curves intersect becomes *defined* in terms of the supply and demand for money, and it no longer makes sense to argue that the rate of interest is *determined* by the supply and demand for loanable funds in any sense that would be recognized by Marshall. But the alternative is to *arbitrarily* assert that the rate of interest will *fall* toward the intersection of Ohlin's *ex ante* supply and demand for loanable-funds curves by way of some sort of magic (i.e., Walrasian *tâtonnement*/recontract process) *without any explanation of any kind as to why it will fall.* And we are still faced with the problem that if expectations change and income falls the *ex-ante* loanable-funds supply curve must shift which will cause the equilibrium rate of interest defined by the intersection of the loanable-funds supply and demand curves to change *before* the market rate of interest can change.

Ohlin's attempted *ex-ante/ex-post* justification of the loanable-funds theory of interest was simply a distraction that has no relevance to the fundamental issue of *causality* raised by Keynes. Ohlin offered no explanation of any kind as to why the rate of interest should respond to his *ex-ante* loanable-funds curves in the *ceteris paribus* situation posed by Keynes, *or in any other situation for that matter*, and, in fact, *no explanation is possible.* The consensus that emerged within the discipline of economics to the effect that Keynes was confused in his criticism of Ohlin having defined his loanable-funds theory in *ex post* terms was a serious mistake in that this consensus arose from an inability to understand the *logical inconsistency* of the loan-able-funds theory with the fundamental principles of supply and demand.[39]

The failure to understand this logical inconsistency misled both Keynesians (e.g., Hansen, 1953, ch.7) and non-Keynesian (e.g., Horwich, ch. X) alike into believing that Keynes' indeterminacy criticism of the classical theory of interest applies to Keynes' own theory as well.  This criticism is as follows:

> For the classical theory...assumes that it can...consider the effect on the rate of interest of (e.g.) a shift in the demand curve for capital, without abating or modifying its assumption as to the amount of the given income out of which the savings are to be made. The independent variables of the classical theory of the rate of interest are the demand curve for capital and the influence of the rate of interest on the amount saved out of a given income; and when (e.g.) the demand curve for capital shifts, the new rate of interest, according to this theory, is given by the point of intersection between the new demand curve for capital and the curve relating the rate of interest to the amounts which will be saved out of the given income. The classical theory of the rate of interest seems to suppose that, if the demand curve for capital shifts or if the curve relating the rate of interest to the amounts saved out of a given income shifts or if both these curves shift, the new rate of interest will be given by the point of intersection of the new positions of the two curves.  But this is a nonsense theory. For the assumption that income is constant is inconsistent with the assumption that these two curves can shift independently of one another. If either of them shift, then, in general, income will change;

---

[39] See Bibow (2000a; 2001).

with the result that the whole schematism based on the assumption of a given income breaks down. (1936, p. 179)

As should be clear from the above, the notion that this criticism of the classical theory applies to Keynes' liquidity-preference theory arises from a failure to understand Keynes' criticism in terms of the basic principles of supply and demand.[40]   It is, of course, true that if either the savings or investment curve shifts the resulting change in income will cause all of these curves to shift (save, perhaps, the supply of money) *over time*, but this is *not* the point of Keynes' criticism.   The point of Keynes' criticism is: "the assumption that income is constant is inconsistent with the assumption that these two curves can shift independently of one another."   *And the issue Keynes is raising here is behavioral*, not *definitional*.

As has been demonstrated above, the only way in which income can remain constant in the face of a *ceteris paribus* shift in either the saving or investment curve is *if the two curves shift in such a way as to make it possible for income to remain constant*.   If there is an increase in the saving curve, for example, the only way income can remain constant is if there is a compensating increase in the *willingness* of producers to increase investment in inventories and otherwise *invest* in maintaining their scale of operations. But if the investment curve shifts in this way there is no reason for the rate of interest to change, and *if the*

---

[40] See Klein (1966, ch. IV) for an example of the kind of confusion embodied in the consensus with regard to this criticism and also Hansen's (1953) exposition of the Keynesian understanding of Keynes for an example of this confusion in the early 1950s.

*investment curve does not shift in this way income must fall "with the result that the whole schematism based on the assumption of a given income breaks down,"* not only because income must change *before* the rate of interest can change, but because if income does change *the savings curve must shift* and the equilibrium rate of interest given by the intersection of the two curves must change *before* the market rate of interest can change.

This criticism most definitely does *not* apply to Keynes' liquidity-preference theory for there is nothing to prevent the market rate of interest from moving to the equilibrium rate of interest implied by the intersection of the supply and demand for money curves in response to a *ceteris paribus* change in the supply or demand for money in Keynes' liquidity-preference theory *given income or any other variable that is assumed to determine the positions of the supply or demand for money curves.*

In the end, the question as to whether or not the rate of interest is determined by saving and investment comes down to this: What does it mean to say that the supply of savings and the demand for investment *determine* the rate of interest in a Marshallian supply and demand curve analysis in a *ceteris paribus* situation in which, given income, an increase in the propensity to save (the supply of loanable funds) must be accompanied by an increase in borrowing (the demand for loanable funds) so that there is no reason for the rate of interest to fall until *after* income falls, and when income does fall the equilibrium rate of interest given by the intersection of these two curves— and toward which the market rate of interest is supposed to move—must change *before* the market rate of interest can change?

We know what it means to argue that a *ceteris paribus* increase in the supply of apples will have a *direct* effect on the price of apples that will cause the price of apples to fall. We also know what it means to argue that the fall in the price of apples will decrease the demands for other fruit as a result of substitution effects that will cause the prices of other fruit to fall. And we know what it means to argue that the *subsequent* fall in the prices of other fruit will have feedback effects on the demand for apples that will reinforce the effect of the increase in the supply of apples on the price of apples through substitution effects on the demand for apples. This argument is understandable because it is possible—through a straightforward Marshallian analysis of supply and demand—to *establish the temporal order in which events must occur* and to work through the processes by which those decision-making units that actually have the *power* to determine prices and quantities interact in markets *through time.*

How would this work if the price of apples were assumed to be determined by the supply and demand for peaches and the price of peaches by the supply and demand for apples? To the extent apples and peaches are substitutes, we would expect, *ceteris paribus*, the quantity of apples demanded to *increase* with an increase in the price of peaches (an upward sloping demand curve) and the quantity of apples supplied to *decrease* (a relatively inelastic downward sloping supply curve). Thus, a *ceteris paribus* increase in the supply of apples at each price of peaches would imply an *increase* in the apple-supply-and-demand equilibrium price of peaches even though there is no reason to expect the price of peaches to change in response to an increase in the supply of apples until *after* there is a change in the price of apples. And when the price of apples does change in response to an increase in the supply of apples we would expect the price of apples to fall which, in turn, we would expect, through substitution effects, to *decrease* the price of peaches, not *increase* the price of peaches as is implied by the *ceteris paribus* increase in the apple-supply-and-demand equilibrium price of peaches.

It would be nonsense to try and explain the dynamic behavior of the prices of apples and peaches through a straightforward Marshallian analysis of supply and demand in this situation or in any situation in which it is assumed that the price of apples is determined by anything other than the supply and demand for apples or that the price of peaches is determined by anything other than the supply and demand for peaches. And, yet, *this is exactly the situation that exists when it is assumed that income is determined by the supply and demand for money or that the rate of interest is determined by saving and investment.*

Keynes demonstrated by way of his old argument that in a monetary economy, that is—*in an economy in which either money or debt (i.e., borrowed money) are required as a medium of exchange*—the entire Marshallian paradigm of supply and demand breaks down if it is assumed that income is determined by anything other than saving and investment or that the rate of interest is determined by anything other than the supply and demand for money. If it is assumed otherwise, the *Marshallian implications with regard to the temporal order in which events must occur are inconsistent with the reality that economic transactions require money or the creation of debt as a medium of exchange.* This means that anyone who argues otherwise must, to paraphrase Ohlin, refute the Marshallian supply and demand curve analysis in *toto* and, in the process, *reject any possibility of being able to provide a logically consistent, causal analysis of dynamic behavior in economics.*

# Chapter III:
# Long-Period Problem of Saving

Keynes made it clear throughout *The General Theory* that his fundamental objection to the classical theory of interest was the way in which this theory was used to justify the belief that an increase in saving will lower the rate of interest and, thereby, increase the rate of capital accumulation and economic wellbeing in the future. It was this belief that Robertson was attempting to justify in his 1936 review of *The General Theory* quoted at length in section **I-a** above as well as in his 1940 summary of the differences between his and Keynes' understandings quoted in section **I-d**.

Keynes was adamantly opposed to the fallacious reasoning on which this belief is based, beginning with Robertson understanding of the short-period problem of saving.

## III-a. Robertson on the Short-Period Problem of Saving

Robertson's understanding of the short-period problem of saving is summarized in the following excerpts from his 1936 review of *The General Theory* quoted at length in section **I-a** above:

> …. Will an increased rate of saving which…takes the form of an increased demand for securities…[and] involves an actual diminution in the rate of expenditure on consumable goods, lead to a progressive shrinkage in total money income?

> ….the increased demand for securities will tend to raise their price….

...some part of the additional savings...will come to rest in the banking accounts of those who, at the higher price of securities, desire to hold an increased quantity of money.... Thus the fall in the rate of interest and the stimulus to the formation of capital will be less...and the stream of money income will tend to contract.

....this is a situation calling for a progressive increase in the supply of money. (1936, pp.187-89)

As is indicated in these excerpts, in Robertson's understanding of this problem an increase in the propensity to save ("increased rate of saving") "which takes the form of an increased demand for securities" will lead to a fall in the rate of interest ("higher price of securities"). This, in turn, will lead to an increase in investment ("formation of capital") and thereby a smooth transfer of resources out of the consumption-goods industries and into the capital-goods industries if facilitated by "a progressive increase in the supply of money" to compensate for the increased demand for speculative balances ("savings...come to rest...in the banking accounts") brought on by the fall in the rate of interest.[41]

This is not the way in which Keynes understood this problem.

### III-b. Keynes on the Short-Period Problem of Saving

As we have seen, Keynes argued that whenever the process of production takes time, at each and every point in time at which a decision must be made concerning employment, output, and income that de-

---

[41] Robertson made this same argument throughout and beyond his controversy with Keynes. See Robertson (1936, pp.187-89; 1940, pp.18-19; 1959, pp.67-70).

cision must be made on the basis of currently held *expectations* with regard to the future. This means that there must be a change in the *expectations* of the producers in the consumption goods industries with regard to the *profitability* of continuing to produce at current levels of employment, output, and income *before* employment, output, and income in the consumption-goods industries can change in response to an increase in the propensity to save. What happens to investment *after* this change in expectations and the resulting fall in income depends not only on the subsequent fall in the rate of interest; *it also depends on how the diminished expectations of profits in the consumption-goods industries affect the subsequent expectations of investors with regard to the prospective yields of further investment in the consumption-goods industries.* Since there is every reason to believe the concomitant fall in the demands for consumption goods will have a *negative* effect on the expectations that determine prospective yields, *there is no a priori reason to believe an increase in the propensity to save will increase the rate of capital accumulation.* As a result, Keynes saw no reason to believe an increase in the propensity to save will lead to an increase in output and economic wellbeing in the future.

Keynes explained his understanding of the nature of this problem in Chapter 8 of *The General Theory*:

> New capital-investment can only take place in excess of current capital-disinvestment if *future* expenditure on consumption is expected to increase.... A diminished propensity to consume to-day can only be accommodated to the public advantage if an increased propensity to consume is expected to exist some day....

> The obstacle to a clear understanding is…an inadequate appreciation of the fact that capital is not a self-subsistent entity existing apart from consumption.  On the contrary, *every weakening in the propensity to consume regarded as a permanent habit must weaken the demand for capital as well as the demand for consumption* [*emphasis* added]. (1936, p. 105-06)

He further expanded on this theme in Chapter 16:

> An act of individual saving means—so to speak—a decision not to have dinner to-day.  But it does not necessitate a decision to have dinner or to buy a pair of boots a week hence or a year hence or to consume any specified thing at any specified date. Thus it depresses the business of preparing to-day's dinner without stimulating the business of making ready for some future act of consumption…. *Moreover, the expectation of future consumption is so largely based on current experience of present consumption that a reduction in the latter is likely to depress the former, with the result that the act of saving will not merely depress the price of consumption-goods and leave the marginal efficiency of existing capital unaffected, but may actually tend to depress the latter also.  In this event it may reduce present investment-demand as well as present consumption-demand* [*emphasis* added].

> If saving consisted not merely in abstaining from present consumption but in placing simultaneously a specific order for future consumption, the effect might indeed be different.... however, an individual decision to save does not, in actual fact, involve the placing of any specific forward order for consumption, but merely the cancellation of a present order.  Thus, *since the expectation of consumption is the only raison d'être of employment, there should be nothing paradoxical in the conclusion that a diminished propensity to con-*

*sume has cet. par. a depressing effect on employment* [*emphasis* added]. (1936, p. 210-11)

Put as simply as possible, Keynes believed that since the ultimate reason for investing in capital goods in the present is to facilitate the production and sale of consumption goods in the future, a fall in the demand for consumption goods in the present that is "regarded as a permanent habit" must reduce the expectations with regard to the demand for consumption goods in the future. This, in turn, can be expected to have a depressing effect on the demand for capital goods in the present, hence, "*cet. par.* a depressing effect on employment," output, and income.

Thus, if you believe, as Keynes believed, that producers must be guided by their *expectations* with regard to the *profitability* of producing at current levels of employment, output, and income there is no reason to believe that employment, output, and income will begin to fall in the consumption-goods industries in response to an increase in saving and subsequently lead to a fall in the rate of interest until *after* there is a change in *expectations* with regard to the *profitability* of continuing to produce in the consumption-goods industries at the current levels of employment, output and income.

If you also believe, as Keynes also believed, that this change in expectations will most likely have an adverse effect on expectations with regard to the *profitability* of further investing in the consumption-goods industries, there is no reason to believe the stimulus to investment that is assumed to arise from the subsequent fall in the rate of interest will not be accompanied by *diminished expectations with regard to the prospective yields that can be expected from increased investment in these industries.*

What happens to the rate of investment in this situation will depend on the interaction between these two forces. Since there is no *a priori* reason to believe the positive effect on investment from the resulting fall in the rate of interest will more than offset the negative effect of the change in expectations on prospective yields there is no reason to believe investment will increase *as this dynamic sequence of events plays itself out.* This is especially so if the concomitant fall in the propensity to consume turns out to be permanent *as expectations adjust to this reality through time.*

What we are talking about here is one of those "complicated partial differentials 'at the back' of several pages of algebra which assume that they all vanish" Keynes warned about in the passage quoted in section **II-a** above, and there can be no doubt where Keynes stood on this issue:

> Thus after giving full weight to the importance of the influence of short-period changes in the state of long-term expectation as distinct from changes in the rate of interest, we are still entitled to return to the latter as exercising, at any rate, in normal circumstances, *a great, though not a decisive*, [*emphasis* added] influence on the rate of investment. (1936, p. 164)

That the rate of interest exercises a great, *though not decisive*, influence on the rate of investment is a central theme of *The General Theory*:

> Even apart from the instability due to speculation, there is the instability due to the characteristic of human nature that a large proportion of our positive activities depend on spontaneous optimism rather than on a mathematical expectation.... Most, probably, of our

decisions to do something positive, the full consequences of which will be drawn out over many days to come, can only be taken as a result of animal spirits— of a spontaneous urge to action rather than inaction, and not as the outcome of a weighted average of quantitative benefits multiplied by quantitative probabilities. Enterprise only pretends to itself to be mainly actuated by the statements in its own prospectus, however candid and sincere…. Thus if the animal spirits are dimmed and the spontaneous optimism falters, leaving us to depend on nothing but a mathematical expectation, enterprise will fade and die;—though fears of loss may have a basis no more reasonable than hopes of profit had before. (1936, pp. 161-62)

Robertson's *ad hoc* analysis of the short-period problem of saving by which he supposed the effects of an increase in saving systematically work their way through the system simply ignored the essential and mercurial role played by expectations in determining the behavior of decision-making units in Keynes' general theory as outlined in the passages quoted above. Nor did Robertson's analysis of the short-period problem of saving in the name of the long-period problem of saving address the fundamental issues raised by Keynes in *The General Theory* with regard to the long-period problem of saving.

### III-c. The Long-Period Problem of Saving

The extent to which Robertson's analysis of the short-period problem of saving failed to address the issues raised by Keynes with regard to the long-period problem of saving can be seen by examining the way in which Robertson ignored what Keynes actually said in "one of his extremer passages (pp. 211-213)" cited by Robertson in his 1936 criticism of Keynes. As was noted in section **I-a** above, in this passage Keynes objected to the "absurd, though almost universal, idea that an act of individual saving is just as good for effective demand as an act of individual consumption... so that current investment is promoted by individual saving to the same extent as present consumption is diminished." According to Keynes:

> It is of this fallacy that it is most difficult to disabuse men's minds. It comes from believing that the owner of wealth desires a capital-asset as such, whereas what he really desires is its prospective yield. Now, prospective yield wholly depends on the expectation of future effective demand in relation to future conditions of supply. If, therefore, an act of saving does nothing to improve prospective yield, it does nothing to stimulate investment... The creation of new wealth wholly depends on the prospective yield of the new wealth reaching the standard set by the current rate of interest....
>
> Nor do we avoid this conclusion by arguing that what the owner of wealth desires is not a given prospective yield but the best available prospective yield.... For this overlooks the fact that there is always an alternative to the ownership of real capital-assets, namely the ownership of money and debts; so that the prospective yield with which the producers of new investment have to be content cannot fall below the standard set by the current rate of interest.... If the reader still finds himself perplexed, let him ask himself why, the quantity of money being unchanged, a fresh act of saving should diminish the sum which it is desired to keep in liquid form at the existing rate of interest. (1936, pp. 211-15) [42]

---

[42] Note that in asking why "a fresh act of saving should diminish the sum which it is desired to keep in liquid form at the existing rate of

In spite of the fact that Robertson chose this "extremer" passage for criticism in the name of the long-period problem of saving, he failed to address directly any of the issues raised by Keynes in this passage with regard to this problem:

1. "the owner of wealth...desires...prospective yield,"

2. "prospective yield depends on the expectation of future effective demand in relation to future conditions of supply,"

3. "If...an act of saving does nothing to improve prospective yield, it does nothing to stimulate investment,"

4. "creation of new wealth wholly depends on the prospective yield of the new wealth reaching the standard set by the current rate of interest,"

5. "there is always an alternative to the ownership of real capital-assets, namely the ownership of money and debts," and

6. "the prospective yield with which the producers of new investment have to be content cannot fall below the standard set by the current rate of interest."

Robertson's 1936 review also failed to address the

---

interest" at the end of this passage Keynes is asking why an increase in saving should diminish the *demand* for money as a store of liquid wealth. There is no reason to believe the demand for money as a store of liquid wealth will change in this situation, and, by virtue of Keynes' old argument, there exists no mechanism by which investment can increase in this *ceteris paribus* situation in the absence of a fall in income or an increase in the supply of money other than through a diminished demand for money as a store of liquid wealth that leads to a fall in the rate of interest. Cf. Blackford (2020, chs. 6 and 7).

fundamental issue raised by Keynes in Chapter 11 of
*The General Theory* with regard to the tendency of
the marginal efficiency of capital to fall as the capital
stock grows:

> If there is an increased investment in any given type
> of capital during any period of time, the marginal effi-
> ciency of that type of capital will diminish as the in-
> vestment in it is increased, partly because the *prospec-
> tive yield will fall as the supply of that type of capital is
> increased*, and partly because, as a rule, pressure on
> the facilities for producing that type of capital will
> cause its supply price to increase; the second of these
> factors being usually the more important in producing
> equilibrium in the short run, but *the longer the period
> in view the more does the first factor take its place*.
> [*emphasis* added] (p. 136)

Robertson failed to acknowledge this issue in his
1936 review in spite of the fact that he had framed his
criticisms in terms of what he called "the long-period
problem of saving," and herein lies the essence of
Keynes' understanding of this problem: "If there is an
increased investment in any given type of capital during any period of time, the marginal efficiency of that
type of capital will diminish as the investment in it is
increased." And it is *essential* to understand that—
contrary to what seems to be the neoclassical understanding of this problem—*the fall in perspective yield
is not simply the result of diminishing returns*. Increasing the stock of any particular kind of capital
good reduces the prospective yield on that particular
kind of capital good even in the absence of diminishing returns in terms of output by way of *the negative
slope of the demand curve for the output that particular kind of capital good produces*.

Herein lies the crux of Keynes' understanding of

the long-period problem of saving—there is a limit to the number of steel mills, automobile factories, gas stations, and Starbucks the economic system can *profitably* support given the state of technology, distribution of income, and the psychological and institutional conditions that constrain the economic system.[43]

The way in which Keynes understood the long-period problem of saving as reflected in the passages quoted above can be summarized as follows:

1.  As saving/investment increases the stock of capital over time, the increasing stock of capital has a tendency to reduce the Marginal Efficiency of Capital (MEC) (i.e., the demand for investment goods) by reducing the *prospective yield* on additional units of various capital assets as these assets become plentiful or even redundant.

2.  The failure of the propensity to save to fall over time (i.e., the propensity to consume to increase) in a way that offsets the negative effects of the fall in the MEC as capital accumulates and prospective yields fall leads to a situation in which a fall in the rate of interest is required in order to achieve the level of investment needed to maintain full employment.

3.  Since the rate of interest is determined by the supply and demand for liquidity and cannot be negative, there are limits to the rate and the extent to which the rate of interest can fall.

---

[43] Cf., Berg et al, Brynjolfsson and McAfee, Deaton, Gordon, Dew-Becker and Gordon, and  Huntington.

4.  To the extent a fall in the rate of interest or propensity to save is unable to offset the effects of the fall in the MEC as saving increases the stock of capital and prospective yields fall over time, the rate of investment must fall below the level needed to maintain full employment.

5.  Given the propensity to save, even if the rate of interest were to adjust rapidly enough to avoid sporadic unemployment in the short run, in the long run the MEC and rate of interest (adjusted for risk and the costs of bringing borrowers and lenders together) must eventually be forced to zero and can fall no more. At this point the economy will stagnate as the fall in output and increase in unemployment force net saving and investment to zero.

This is the way Keynes' viewed the long-period problem of saving—a dynamic struggle between the forces that determine saving, investing, capital accumulation, prospective yield, and the rate of interest—a struggle that must play itself out *through time.*

In the passage quoted in section **I-d** above, Robertson asserted that the net result of his decision to save rather than spend money on new clothes will be "an increase, *perhaps* [*emphasis* added], in capital outlay.[1]" And in the accompanying footnote he states: "[1]Even this is not certain, since the demand of the tailor, weaver, etc., for machines will decline." This is, of course, precisely the issue raised by Keynes in the passages quoted in section **III-b** above, and by 1940 it appeared that this had finally registered with Robertson. In retelling this tale in his 1959 *Lectures* (pp. 67-70), however, it had apparently unregistered as Robertson reverted to his original 1936 position in which the potential effects of an increase in saving on expectations, prospective yields, and the demand for capital goods were again ignored.

While Robertson was unimpressed with the causal/dynamic nature of Keynes' analysis of the short-period problem of saving, Robertson was at least aware of the long-run problem emphasized by Keynes. This is indicated by Robertson's discussion of the "liquidity trap" in his *Essays*, (1940, pp. 33-9) and in his discussion of "The Stagnation Thesis" in his *Lectures*. (1959, pp. 59-76) At the same time, Robertson was either unable or unwilling to make the connection between the short-period and long-period problems as he continued to ignore the effects of the fall in the propensity to consume on prospective yields in his analysis of the short-period problem, save for the fleeting reference in the footnote cited above, and he was either unable to, or simply unwilling to follow the argument through to its logical conclusion.

## III-d. Neoclassical Consensus on Keynes

Keynes was not at all sanguine with regard to the ability of *laissez-faire* to cope with the fallout from the long-period problem of saving:

> What would this involve for a society which finds itself so well equipped with capital that its marginal efficiency is zero and would be negative with any additional investment; yet possessing a monetary system, such that money will 'keep' and involves negligible costs of storage and safe custody, with the result that in practice interest cannot be negative; and, in conditions of full employment, disposed to save?

> If, in such circumstances, we start from a position of full employment, entrepreneurs will necessarily make

losses if they continue to offer employment on a scale which will utilize the whole of the existing stock of capital. Hence the stock of capital and the level of employment will have to shrink until the community becomes so impoverished that the aggregate of saving has become zero.... Thus for a society such as we have supposed, the position of equilibrium, under conditions of *laissez-faire*, will be one in which employment is low enough and the standard of life sufficiently miserable to bring savings to zero. More probably there will be a cyclical movement round this equilibrium position. For if there is still room for uncertainty about the future, the marginal efficiency of capital will occasionally rise above zero leading to a 'boom', and in the succeeding 'slump' the stock of capital may fall for a time below the level which will yield a marginal efficiency of zero in the long run. Assuming correct foresight, the equilibrium stock of capital which will have a marginal efficiency of precisely zero will, of course, be a smaller stock than would correspond to full employment of the available labor; for it will be the equipment which corresponds to that proportion of unemployment which ensures zero saving.[44]

Nor was Keynes confident that the fallout from the long-period problem of saving could be effectively managed with monetary policy alone. At the end of Chapter 13 he wrote:

> For my own part I am now somewhat skeptical of the success of a merely monetary policy directed towards influencing the rate of interest. I expect to see the State, which is in a position to calculate the marginal

---

[44] The situation described by Keynes in this passage clearly existed in the United States in depths of the Great Depression as net investment became negative and the capital stock fell from 1931 through 1935. (See Keynes (Sept. 1936).)

efficiency of capital-goods on long views and on the basis of the general social advantage, taking an ever greater responsibility for directly organising investment; since it seems likely that the fluctuations in the market estimation of the marginal efficiency of different types of capital…will be too great to be offset by any practicable changes in the rate of interest.  (p.164)

In Chapter 22 he declared:

In conditions of *laissez-faire* the avoidance of wide fluctuations in employment may, therefore, prove impossible without a far reaching change in the psychology of investment markets such as there is no reason to expect, I conclude that the duty of ordering the current volume of investment cannot safely be left in private hands. (p. 320)

And in the final chapter of *The General Theory* Keynes concluded:

…it seems unlikely that the influence of banking policy on the rate of interest will be sufficient by itself to determine an optimum rate of investment. I conceive, therefore, that *a* somewhat *comprehensive socialisation of investment will prove the only means of securing an approximation to full employment* [*emphasis* added]; (1936, p. 378)

Thus, Keynes believed that, given the instability of the psychology of investment markets, a system of *laissez-faire* guided by monetary policy alone would not be able to deal effectively with the long-period problem of saving, and that maintaining full employment in the future would require "a somewhat comprehensive socialisation of investment."  This conclusion was not embraced by the Keynesians following World War II.

The controversy that arose from Keynes' publication of *The General Theory* focused on Robertson's criticisms of Keynes in terms of the short-period problem while the long-period problem was treated as being of secondary importance. In addition, the Keynesians viewed the economic prosperity that followed the war as a validation of their neoclassical economics as seen through the eyes of Hicks. As a result, Keynes' analysis of the long-period problem of saving did not become an integral part of the neoclassical consensus that emerged in the 1960s with regard to the nature of Keynes' fundamental contributions to economic thought.[45] This created a situation in which the effects of an increasing propensity to save and the accumulation of capital on the *prospective yield* of additional increases in the stock of capital were not incorporated into the world-view of policy makers leading up to the Crash of 2008 to the effect that their view of reality contained a vision of the economic system in which monetary policy could be used through its effects on the rate of interest and investment to main-

---

[45] This was because of the inability or, perhaps, unwillingness of economists to understand or to explain the reasons for the Great Depression and economic prosperity that followed World War II in terms of Keynes' general theory that can be seen in such works as Samuelson's *Economics*, Hansen's *Guide to Keynes*, and eventually in Klein's 1966, *The Keynesian Revolution*, works which provide little more than a caricature of Keynes' *General Theory*. As a result, there was very little Keynes to be found in Keynesian economics by the 1960s. See Clower, Crotty (1980), Davidson, Minsky, Leijonhufvud, and cf., Klein (1966).

With regard to unwillingness it must be noted that there was a considerable ideological and political backlash against popularizing Keynes' conclusions in the United States during Communist witch hunts of the House Un-American Activities Committee in the 1940s that evolved into the McCarthy Era in the 1950s. See Boyer and Morais, Giraud, Johnson (2006).

tain full employment indefinitely into the future.

This is a vision that is fully consistent with Robertson's belief that all that is needed to solve the short-period problem of saving is "a progressive increase in the supply of money." It is also a vision that, if carried to its logical conclusion, presupposes monetary policy can be effective in maintaining full employment by lowering the rate of interest and thereby stimulating investment even if the entire country were to become paved over with concrete and every square inch of land were to sport a factory or high-rise apartment building.[46]

As has been noted, Keynes did not share this vision of the economic system in that he did not believe monetary policy alone would be able to solve the long-period problem of saving. It is sobering to realize that Keynes has, in fact, proved to be prophetic in this regard as we have seen monetary policy effectively lower rates of interest in the midst of speculative bubbles almost continuously since the early 1980s throughout the Great Moderation on our way to the Crash of 2008 and the secular stagnation that followed. As we shall see, *this is exactly the result that would have been expected from the economic policies put in place leading up to the Crash of 2008 and the economic stagnation that followed if Keynes' analysis of the long-period problem of saving had been clearly understood.*

---

[46] Cf., Hayes (p.54). It is also a vision that ignores the way in which skill- and capital-biased technological change, combined with the proliferation of winner-take-all markets, can render much of the labor supply redundent in the manner examined by Brynjolfsson and McAfee and the limits to technology based growth examined by Gordon, and Dew-Becker and Gordon.

# Chapter IV:
# Long-Period Problem of Debt

Keynes did not present his general theory as a system of simultaneous equations. That was done by John Hicks, Paul Samuelson, Gardner Ackley, Don Patinkin, and countless other Keynesians. Their approach was Walrasian, and as a result of their efforts a Walrasian revolution took place in economics following Keynes' publication of *The General Theory of Employment, Interest, and Money*. This revolution took Keynes' name in spite of the fact that Keynes was a *protégé* of Marshall, not Walras, and in spite of the fact that Keynes emphatically rejected the kind of mathematical approach to economics that ignores "the complexities and interdependencies of the real world" implicit in the Walrasian methodology.[47]

The single most important reason for the failure to understand the causal/dynamic nature of Keynes' theory of interest and, beyond this, to understand the causal/dynamic nature of Keynes' method of analysis

---

[47] See Keynes (1936, pp. 297-8) quoted in section **II-a** above. Skidelsky (2003, ch. 30) explained the way in which this revolution took place and the extent to which "Keynes acquiesced...for pedagogical and policy purposes" (p. 547) while at the same time resisted it. As was noted in **Chapter I**, the LP/LF debate more or less ended as the Keynesians stopped responding to the anti-Keynesians after Robertson's death in 1963. As it turned out, by the end of the 1970s Keynes had effectively lost the debate as the loanable-funds theory became mainstream again and began to reappear in textbooks as the Walrasian paradigm with its *tâtonnement*/recontract dynamics became the dominant paradigm within the discipline of economics. See Asimakopulos, Bibow, Clower (1975), Crotty (1980, 1990), Fleisher and Kopecky, Leijonhufvud, Stiglitz (1999), Terzi, Tsiang (1980), and Wray.

in *The General Theory* itself is the perpetual attempt to force Keynes into a Walrasian mold. Keynes simply cannot be understood from this perspective. Keynes' method of analysis was *causal* and *dynamic*, just as was Marshall's, and the only way to understand Keynes is to think in terms of Marshall's "organized and orderly method of thinking out particular problems" rather than the "method of blind manipulation" of Walras.[48]

As we have seen, the fundamental issues that separated Robertson and Keynes with regard to the theory of interest arose from the incompatibility of the savings-investment/loanable-funds theory with the Marshallian paradigm of supply and demand. This incompatibility follows directly from Keynes' old argument in his *Treatise on Money* to the effect that an increase in saving cannot *in itself* cause an increase in the prices of assets, and it must be emphasized that this argument is unquestionably valid. As has been noted above, the validity of this argument was acknowledged by Robertson on at least four separate occasions, and no one has demonstrated, or even claimed to have demonstrated that this argument is invalid.

In spite of this fact, the implications of Keynes' argument have not been well received within the discipline of economics. The typical attitude is epitomized by the following response by Don Patinkin to

---

[48] The Marshallian roots of Keynes' dynamic methodology were, of course, understood by such writers as Hicks (1946, pp. 3-4) and Johnson (1961, pp. 2-6), the difference being that Hicks saw this as a strength and Johnson as a weakness, and neither dealt with the issue of *direct causality* that lies at the core of Marshall's *ceteris paribus* methodology. See also Clower.

Hugh Rose's (1959) denial of the validity of Walras' law:

> Mr. Rose's comment relates to a point which is quite incidental to my main argument. Furthermore, it is based on an uncritical application of one of Bent Hansen's remarks about the nature of Walras'[3] Law. The essence of these remarks is that if the demand for loans (or any other good) is defined in the (unusual) *ex-post* sense, while the demand for money is defined in the (usual) *ex-ante* sense, then the excess demand for money is not equal to the value of the excess supply of other goods. This is certainly not surprising. But I do have difficulty in understanding the meaning and significance of an argument which mixes *ex-ante* and *ex-post* quantities in this way. (1959, p. 254-5)

This response is typical in that Patinkin acknowledged the validity of Hansen's (hence, Rose's) remarks ("this is certainly not surprising") and then dismissed these remarks out of hand ("I do have difficulty in understanding the meaning and significance of an argument which mixes *ex-ante* and *ex-post* quantities in this way.")

The reason for the difficulty in understanding an argument which mixes *ex-ante* and *ex-post* quantities in this way is that such arguments are meaningless within the context of the Walrasian paradigm with its *tâtonnement*/recontract dynamics. The question with which Keynes' old argument is concerned is whether or not an increase in saving can, *in itself*, have a *direct* effect on the prices of assets—that is, it has to do with *causality*. Within the context of Keynes' general theory this question reduces to whether or not it makes sense to assume the rate of interest is determined by savers and investors by way of the supply and demand for loanable funds. As we have seen, this question cannot be answered within the context of the Walrasian paradigm. It can only be answered within the context of the Marshallian paradigm.

The fundamental difference between these two paradigms is that when the economic system is viewed from the perspective of Walras—choices made simultaneously and constrained by income so that markets achieve equilibrium by way of a mythical auctioneer—the result is an analytic framework that is descriptive and static within which it is not possible to provide a logically consistent, causal explanation as to how the economic system changes through time.[49]

When the economic system is viewed from the perspective of Marshall the result is an analytic framework that is *causal* and *dynamic* within which it is possible to provide a logically consistent, causal explanation as to how the economic system changes through time.[50]

Marshall's methodology may not be mathematically tractable or elegant, which undoubtedly accounts for its lack of appeal to mathematical purists, but it does provide a coherent analytical framework in which it is possible to establish the *temporal order in which events must occur* and, thus, to separate *cause* and *effect*—an analytical framework in which it is possible to explain the way in which the economic system *changes* in terms of the actual choices available to, and the motivations of those decision-making units

---

[49] Cf., the approach of Clower, Leijonhufvud, Barro and Grossman, Grossman, and Blackford (1975; 1976) wherein choices are assumed to be constrained by realized income when markets fail to clear which results in a quasi-Walrasian, static analysis of market disequilibrium.

[50] See Blackford (2020, ch. 6).

that actually have the *power* to *cause* the economic system to change.

Not only did this methodology make it possible for Keynes to formulate a general theory in which all prices and quantities are determined by way of the fundamental constructs of supply and demand which lie at the core of Marshall's theory of value,[51] it also made it possible for Keynes to provide a logically consistent, *causal* explanation of the Great Depression, something the classical economics of his time was unable to do, constrained as it was by the assumption that the rate of interest is determined by savers and investors. This same methodology also makes it possible to provide a logically consistent, *causal* explanation of the Great Recession, something the neoclassical economics of our time is unable to do, constrained as it is by the Walrasian budget constraint.

### IV-a. The Fruits of Marshall's Methodology

In applying Marshall's methodology to "the complexities and interdependencies of the real world," Keynes was able to obtain a number of critical insights as to how the economic system works on his way to *The General Theory of Employment, Interest, and Money*. These insights have been discussed throughout the text above and can be summarized as follows:

1.  The ultimate justification for production in a market economy is to satisfy the demands of consumers.

2.  The truly causal variables in an economy in which the process of production takes time are expectations with regard to the future.

---

[51] See Blackford (2020, ch. 6).

3. The willingness to invest in real assets depends on the prospective yield of those assets—that is, the yield investors *expect* to receive in the future as a result of investing in those assets.

4. Prospective yields are affected not only by the rate of interest (which affects the cost of investing in real assets) but also by the stocks of real assets relative to the demand for the outputs those assets produce (which affect expectations with regard to the proceeds that can be obtained from *increases* in the stocks of real assets) as well as by the infamous "animal spirits" that take the investor beyond the limits of rational calculation.

5. The rate of interest is a purely monetary phenomenon, determined by the supply and demand for money as rates of interest adjust to equate wealth-holders' demands for liquidity with the existing stocks of assets.

6. Monetary policy is limited in its ability to affect rates of interest by the propensities of wealth holders with regard to their demands for liquidity and the ability of the monetary authority to affect the existing stocks of assets available to meet their demands.

7. Given the existing stocks of assets and the rates of interest determined by the propensities of wealth holders, the level of economic activity is determined by the effective demands for consumption and investment goods—that is, by the proceeds producers *expect* to receive as they maximize their *expectation* of profits through the employment of resources.

8. Since the ultimate justification for production is to

satisfy the demands of consumers, and since the ultimate purpose of investment is to increase the production of consumption goods in the future, the demand for investment goods is ultimately determined by *expectations* with regard to future consumption.

9. And since expectations with regard to future consumption are largely determined by current consumption, the effective demands for consumption and investment goods (hence, the level of economic activity) are largely determined by current consumption.

These insights drove Keynes to the inescapable conclusion that *consumption is the driving force for economic growth and employment, not saving*:

> For we have seen that, up to the point where full employment prevails, the growth of capital depends not at all on a low propensity to consume but is, on the contrary, held back by it; and only in conditions of full employment is a low propensity to consume conducive to the growth of capital. (Keynes, 1936, p. 372-73)[52]

---

[52] It is worth noting at this point that Robertson's obsession with Keynes' "concession to the efficacy of Thrift under conditions of full employment (p. 112)" clearly indicates the extent of Robertson's inability, or unwillingness to understand Keynes'argument in this regard. The passage Robertson cites is as follows:

> Thus, after all, the actual rates of aggregate saving and spending do not depend on Precaution, Foresight, Calculation, Improvement, Independence, Enterprise, Pride or Avarice. Virtue and vice play no part. It all depends on how far the rate of interest is favourable to investment, after taking account of the marginal efficiency of capital[1]. No, this is an overstatement. *If the rate of interest were so governed as to maintain continuous full employment* [*emphasis* added], virtue would resume her sway;—the rate of capital accumulation would depend on the weakness of the propensity to con-

Given the force of Keynes' arguments, this conclusion would appear to be rather straightforward and irrefutable. And, yet, it seems to have had very little impact on economic policy leading up to the Crash of 2008.

Over the thirty-five years leading up to the Crash of 2008 we managed to a) encourage individual and municipal retirement accounts and funds, b) convert Social Security from a pay-as-you-go to a partial-prepayment system, c) neglect the minimum wage while emasculating labor unions, d) cut corporate taxes and taxes on the wealthy while increasing taxes on the not so wealthy, e) weaken usury laws while enacting draconian bankruptcy laws, f) refuse to enforce antitrust laws, g) reduce investment in physical infrastructure and human capital, and h) dismantle our domestic and international financial regulatory sys-

---

sume. Thus, once again, the tribute that classical economists pay to her is due to their concealed assumption that the rate of interest always is so governed. (Keynes, 1937, p. 111-12)

This is hardly a "concession to the efficacy of Thrift under conditions of full employment." The purpose of Keynes' *General Theory* is to explain why the rate of interest is *not* "always so governed as to maintain continuous full employment," not to deny the truism that if it were possible for the system to be kept at full employment the rate of capital accumulation must, by definition, increase with an increase in the propensity to consume. Keynes clearlly understood what Robertson did not, namely, that in the absence of an increase in the demand for investment goods an increase in thrift will have a negative effect on investment, employment, output, and inccome by diminishing the demand for consumption goods whether the system is at full employment or not. See Keynes (1936, chs. 11, 12, and 22).

The only way in which an individual act of saving can directly increase investment, whether the system is at full employment or not, is if it takes the form of a purchase of, or the production of a newly produced capital good, that is, *if it takes the form of investment*. It is *investment* that increases the stock of capital, not saving. Saving and investment may, by definition, be equal, but they are not the same thing.

tems.[53]  These are policies that enhance the aggregate propensity to save by increasing the concentration of income and facilitating trade deficits—*policies that only make sense in macroeconomic models that ignore the long-run relationship between consumption and effective demand and assume that saving enhances economic growth and employment.*

Of particular importance in this regard is the abandonment in 1973 of the capital controls embodied in the *managed* international exchange system negotiated by Keynes at Bretton Woods in 1944 and replacing it with what became known as the Washington Consensus which promoted unrestricted international finance and trade.  This eventually led to bilateral trade agreements with China after Nixon's historic visit in 1972, the North American Free Trade Agreement in 1994, and our joining the World Trade Organization in 1995.[54]

The policies implemented over the thirty-five years leading up to the Crash of 2008 changed the *institutional structure* of our economic system in a way that led to a dramatic decrease in our international balance of trade (**Figure 4**) which was mostly positive following World War II through the mid 1970s, and had fallen to a deficit equal to 5% of GDP by 2007.  These institutional changes also led to a decoupling of the growth of wages and productivity in the economic system (**Figure 5**) which facilitated a dramatic increase in the concentration of income (**Figure 6**) as the income share of the top 1% of the

---

[53] See Blackford (2018) and Crotty (2009).

[54] See Bair, Blackford (2018), Crotty (2002), Klein (2007), and Rodrik.

## Figure 4: Net Exports, 1929-2017.

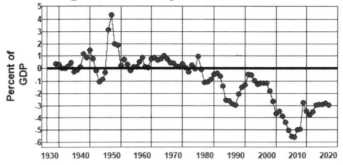

Source: Bureau of Economic Analysis, Table 1.1.5.

## Figure 5: Labor Productivity and Compensation, 1950-2017.

Source: Bureau of Labor Statistics, Productivity and Costs.

## Figure 6: Income Share of Top and Bottom of the Income Distribution, 1920-2014.

Source: World Wealth and Income Database.

income distribution increased from 8% of total income 1975 to 23% by 2007, and the income share of the bottom 90% fell from 69% of total income to 53%. The result was an increase in saving in the foreign sector (by way of our increased trade deficits) and at the top of the income distribution in the private sector (by way of the increased concentration of income and higher propensity to save at the top of the income distribution).[55]

## IV-b. Buildup to the Crash of 2008

One would have expected the changes in the balance of trade and distribution of income in **Figure 4** and **Figure 6** to have had a disruptive effect on employment and output as prices and profits fell in those industries that produce for those at the bottom of the income distribution as well as in those industries that compete with imports. This is especially the case for industries that utilized mass-production technologies which require mass markets—that is, markets with large numbers of people with purchasing power—to be viable.

The more than doubling of the income share of the top 1% of the income distribution from 1975 through 2007 created a situation in which the bottom 99% of the income distribution—99 out of 100 families—had, on average, 16% less purchasing power out of income relative to the output produced in 2007 than the bottom 99% had relative to the output produced in 1975, and as we go down the income distribution the reduction in purchasing power out of in-

---

[55] See also Alperovitz, Blackford (2018, chs. 1-3), Cynamon, Galbraith (2012, 2008), Hartmann, Kuttner, Kwak, Lansley, Madrick, Piketty, Reich, and Stiglitz (2015, 2012).

come becomes even more dramatic. The fall in the income share of the bottom 90% was 23%. This means that in 2007 the bottom 90% of the income distribution—9 out of 10 families—had, on average, 23% less purchasing power out of income relative to the output produced in 2007 than the bottom 90% had in 1975 relative to the output produced in 1975.

This increase in the concentration of income undermined our domestic mass markets and, hence, mass-production producers, a situation that was made worse as international deficits grew and a larger portion of domestic income was spent on foreign goods than was generated by sales to foreigners. But even though the increase in the concentration of income and international deficits had devastating effects in the manufacturing sector of our economy (as was to be expected and as the decline in the rust-belt states can attest) and in spite of three minor recessions we experienced from 1980 through 2006, the unemployment rate trended downward over this period as employment rose leading up to the Crash of 2008:

**Figure 7: Unemployment Rate, 1929-2017.**

Source: Bureau of Labor Statistics (1),
*Economic Report of the President,* 1966 (D17).

At the same time, mass market retailers such as Wal-Mart, Amazon, and Home Depot seem to have thrived.

Maintaining the full employment of our resources in this situation requires that the increase in saving in the foreign sector and at the top of the income distribution in the private sector be offset, either through a) a decrease in saving in some other part of the system or b) through an increase in investment. The way in which this was actually accomplished over the twenty-seven years leading up to the Crash of 2008 was through a) an increase in dissaving in the public sector and at the bottom of the income distribution in the private sector and b) an increase in investment as a result of speculative bubbles in the junk bond and commercial real estate markets in the 1980s, in the markets for tech stocks in the 1990s, and in the housing markets in the 2000s.[56]

Given the dramatic institutional changes that occurred over this period of time, these offsets to the increase in saving in the foreign sector and at the top of the income distribution in the private sector were accompanied by a continual increase in debt relative to income as total domestic debt in the United States increased from 165% of GDP in 1980 to 364% by 2008. In 2008 the GDP stood at $14.7 trillion and the total debt at $53.6 trillion. Debt of this magnitude places a huge burden on the system through the transfer of income and wealth from debtors to creditors. Even an

---

[56] See Acharya and Richardson, Bair, Baker, Bibow (2009), Black, Blackford (2018), Blanchard et al, Bordo, Cohan, Cooper, Crotty (2009), Cynamon and Fazzari, Farmer, FCIC, FDIC, Freeman, Galbraith (2008, 2012), Garcia et al., Gelinas, Iacoviello, Johnson and Kwak, Klein (2007), Krugman, Kumhof et al, Lansley, Levin and Coburn, Lewis, Lowenstein, Mian and Sufi, Morelli and Atkinson, Morris, Palley, Phillips, Reinhart, Carmon and Rogoff, Reich, Rodrik, Roubini and Mihm, Skidelsky (2012), Summers, Stewart, Stiglitz (2010, 2012), Taleb, Wessel, and Zinman.

average interest rate as low as 3% would require an annual transfer equal to 11% of GDP when total debt is as high as 364% of GDP as it was in 2008. An average interest rate of 5% would require an annual transfer equal to 18% of GDP:

**Figure 8: Total, Non-Federal, and Federal Debt, 1920-2016.**

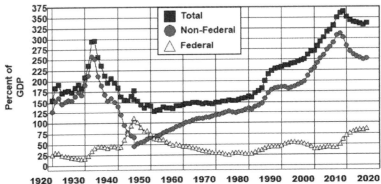

Source: Federal Reserve (L1), Historical Statistics of the U.S. (Cj870, Cj872, Ca10), Bureau of Economic Analysis Table 1.1.5.57

Even more ominous is the fact that non-federal domestic debt more than doubled relative to income from 1980 through 2008, increasing from 139% of GDP to 321%.[58]    Unlike the federal government (which has the constitutional right to print money to pay its debts) those entities that make up the non-federal sector of the domestic economy—individuals,

---

[57] See Blackford (2018, ch. 3 and its appendix) for an explanation of the way in which the graph in **Figure 8** was constructed.

[58] See Acharya, Bair, Bibow (2009), Baker, Bernanke, Blackford (2018, chs. 4-8, 10), Bruner, Cohan, Cooper, Crotty (2009), Eichengreen, Farmer, FCIC, FDIC, Levin and Coburn, Fisher, Friedman and Schwartz, Galbraith (2008, 2012), Garcia et al., Gelinas, Graeber, Johnson and Kwak, Kindleberger, Klein (2007), Lewis, Lowenstein, MacKay, Mian and Sufi, Meltzer, Minsky, Morris, Palley, Perino, Phillips, Reinhart and Rogoff, and Reich.

businesses, and municipal governments—must service their debt out of income. When they cannot service their debt out of income they must borrow to do so. Barring the ability to borrow, they are forced to either sell assets in an attempt to obtain the *money* needed to meet their financial obligations, or they are forced to default on those obligations—the kinds of selling of assets and defaults that lead to financial crises. (Minsky)

Non-federal debt of this magnitude makes the economic system extremely vulnerable, and when much of that debt is the product of speculative bubbles and backed by assets and incomes generated by speculative bubbles the situation becomes perilous. It should not have been a surprise that the upturn in interest rates that began in 2005 in response to the Federal Reserve's attempt to moderate the housing bubble while refusing to regulate the mortgage market sent shockwaves throughout the financial system in 2007 as the prime rate rose from 4.3% in 2004 to 6.2% in 2005 to 8.0% in 2006 and remained at 8.0% into 2007.[59]

It also should not have been a surprise that the bursting of the housing bubble in the United States reverberated throughout the rest of the world as the economic policies that led to the deregulation of our financial system and the international imbalance at home were not an exclusively American phenomenon. They had been promulgated all over the world by institutions such as the International Monetary Fund in the name of the Washington Consensus. The result

---

[59] Economic Report of the President, 2013, Table B-73, p. 410.

was not only financial deregulation, international deficits, and a real estate bubble financed by expanding debt relative to income in the United States but in many countries in Europe and elsewhere around the world as well.[60] As a result, the crisis that began in the American financial system in 2007 was destined to create a worldwide economic catastrophe.

## IV-c. The Long-Period Problem of Debt

The economic stagnation in the United States that followed the Crash of 2008 is easily understood in terms of Keynes' long-period problem of saving:

1.  The institutional changes that occurred over the thirty-five years leading up to the crash increased saving a) in the foreign sector by way of increasing international deficits, b) at the top of the income distribution by way of the increase in the concentration of income, and c) in general by way of policies that encourage private- and public-sector saving (such as encouraging private and municipal retirement accounts and funds and converting Social Security from a pay-as-you-go to a partial-prepayment system). The result was an increase in the aggregate propensity to save that was partially offset by *dissaving* in the rest of the private and public sectors as interest rates fell and *the capital stock grew* in the midst of speculative bubbles.

2.  The persistence of international deficits (foreign-sector saving) and the concentration of income after the crash, combined with the unwillingness of the federal government to sufficiently increase deficits and the reduction in dissaving and increase in

---

[60] See Blackford (2018), FCIC, Klein (2007), and Rodrik.

saving in a large portion of the private sector, bolstered the aggregate propensity to save.

3. The increased aggregate propensity to save and lack of speculative bubbles to generate investment and income in the way in which speculative bubbles had generated investment and income as the capital stock grew during the twenty-five years leading up to the crash led to a reduction in the rate of growth of consumption.

4. The reduction in the rate of growth of consumption, combined with the increase in the capital stock leading up to the crash diminished prospective yields and the willingness to invest.

5. The inability of interest rates to continue to fall in this situation led to the economic stagnation that followed in the wake of the crash.

Explaining the buildup to the crash and the crash itself, however, takes us beyond Keynes' analysis of the long-period problem of saving.

While Keynes analyzed the long-period problem of saving in intricate detail throughout the *General Theory*, one aspect of this problem he did not examine in intricate detail is the role played by the flow of loanable funds in the economic system. Even though this flow does not determine the rate of interest (as Keynes clearly understood), *the flow of loanable funds changes the stock of debt in the economic system over time just as the flow of investment changes the stock of capital in the economic system over time.* And even though changes in neither the stock of capital nor the stock of debt affect the system in a significant way in the short-run, *both can have dramatic effects on the system in the long run.*

There is nowhere to be found in Keynes an analysis of the relationship between the flow of loanable funds and the accumulation of debt comparable to that of his analysis of the relationship between the flow of investment and the accumulation of capital in spite of the fact that:

1. The creation of debt plays an essential role in achieving an efficient allocation and employment of economic resources by providing a mechanism through which purchasing power can be transferred from those who have it and are unwilling to spend to those who do not have it and are willing borrow in order to spend.

2. At the same time, the most serious depressions involve financial crises that have at their root the inability to service debt.[61]

3. If the *institutions* of society are such that given the state of technology the resulting distribution of income and balance of trade requires an increase in debt relative to income in order to maintain full employment in the short run eventually debt service must overwhelm the system and cause a financial crisis that will make it impossible to sustain full employment in the long run.[62]

Even though Keynes did not examine this problem explicitly, the nature of this problem is easily understood within the analytic framework of Keynes' general theory.[63]

---

[61] See Blackford (2018, ch. 10), Crotty (2009), Fisher (1932), Min sky, and Reinhart and Rogoff.

[62] See Blackford (2018, chs. 3, 4, and 10).

[63] Cf., Minsky (1992).

Since the level of employment is determined by effective demand (that is, by the *proceeds* producers *expect* to receive as they maximize their *expectation* of profits from the employment of resources) in Keynes' general theory, *equilibrium* in employment, output, and income requires that the rate at which decision-making units choose to spend money to purchase the output employers choose to produce must be equal to the proceeds producers expect to receive at the given level of employment. If the chosen rate of expenditure is greater than producers expect to receive, producers will be motivated to increase their profits by increasing employment, output, and income as their expectations adjust to this reality. Similarly, if the chosen rate of expenditure is less than producers expect to receive, producers will be motivated to increase their profits (or decrease their losses) by decreasing employment, output, and income as their expectations adjust to this reality.

This mechanism by which the equilibrium levels of employment, output, and income are assumed to be achieved and maintained presents a problem: In general, individual decision-making units seldom spend all of their income on currently produced domestic output. Some income is spent on goods from foreign producers (imports), some to purchase financial and real assets that are not part of current output, and some simply accrues and is not paid out or is deposited in banks and allowed to just sit there. In addition, some income is directly lent to those who are willing to borrow (for whatever reason) and some is used to repay previously accumulated debt.

These kinds of dispositions of current income are not expenditures on currently produced domestic output, and to the extent they lead to expenditures out of current income falling short of the proceeds producers expect to receive, expenditures out of current income must be compensated for in some way if equilibrium in employment, output, and income is to be maintained. This can be accomplished either through purchases by foreigners (exports) or by other decision-making units choosing to spend an offsetting amount of money on current output in *excess* of their income, that is, by other decision-making units selling real or financial assets, spending previously accrued income that is paid out and taking money just sitting in the bank out of the bank, or by borrowing money which is used to purchase currently produced domestic output in such a way as to satisfy the expectations of domestic producers.

Even though there are many ways by which these offsetting compensations take place, the most important are the creation of debt and the purchase and sale of newly issued equities. Both of these mechanisms play a crucial role in transferring purchasing power within the system from those who have it and do not wish to spend to those who do not have it and do wish to spend, especially when it comes to financing investment.

Of these two mechanisms, *the most critical is the creation of debt* by way of an increase in direct loans or over drafts to decision-making units, an increase in trade credit, or through newly created debt instruments such as mortgages, bonds, notes, bills, repurchase agreements, commercial credit, etc. Debt is most critical because, unlike the other offsets, debt entails interest and repayment obligations which have the potential to seriously disrupt the functioning of the entire economic system if these obligations cannot be met.[64]

To the extent borrowed money is used to purchase newly produced goods and services that would not have been purchased otherwise the resulting debt facilitates the demand for goods and services and, thereby, facilitates employment, output, and income. This is perfectly normal and is an essential mechanism by which the system functions, but this is not the only way debt is created. Debt is also created for the purpose of purchasing used and financial assets for practical as well as speculative purposes, and debt can become self-generating in what Hyman Minsky referred to as "Ponzi finance" (1992)—a situation in which debt cannot be serviced out of income and must increase as debtors are forced to borrow in order to pay the interest on their debt and to refinance the principal when repayment comes due. If the institutions within society are such that, given the state of technology, the rate at which debt must be created in order to sustain full employment is greater than the rate at which income increases full employment cannot be maintained in the absence of an increase in debt relative to income. As was noted above, a continually increasing debt relative to income is unsustainable in the long run as it leads to a situation in which debt service must eventually overwhelm the

---

[64] See Acharya and Richardson, Baker, Bibow (2009) Blackford (2018), Blanchard et al, Bordo and Meissner, Cohan, Cooper, Crotty (2009), Dowd and Hutchinson, FCIC, FDIC, Gelinas, Iacoviello, Johnson and Kwak, Fisher, Kindleberger, Kumhof et al, Levin and Coburn, Mian and Sufi, Lewis, Lowenstein, Mian and Sufi, Morelli and Atkinson, Minsky, Morris, Palley, Phillips, Reich, Reinhart and Rogoff, Rodrik, Roubini and Mihm, Stewart, Stiglitz (2010), and Zinman.

system.

It is fairly obvious that herein lies the cause of major financial crises and recessions,[65] and, yet, not only was the relationship between consumption and economic growth and employment ignored by policy makers leading up to the Crash of 2008, the circumstances in which the *institutions* within society are such that full employment can be maintained only through an increase in debt relative to income was ignored as well in spite of the fact that *this was exactly the situation that existed leading up to the Crash of 2008 and the economic stagnation that followed.*[66]

---

[65] See Acharya and Richardson, Baker, Bibow (2009) Blackford (2018), Blanchard et al, Bordo and Meissner, Cohan, Cooper, Crotty (2009), Dowd and Hutchinson, FCIC, FDIC, Gelinas, Iacoviello, Johnson and Kwak, Fisher, Kindleberger, Kumhof et al, Levin and Coburn, Mian and Sufi, Lewis, Lowenstein, Mian and Sufi, Morelli and Atkinson, Minsky, Morris, Palley, Phillips, Reich, Reinhart and Rogoff, Rodrik (2014), Roubini and Mihm, Stewart, Stiglitz (2010), and Zinman.

[66] This was also the situation leading up to the Crash of 1929 and the Great Depression that followed. Robert Reich provides the following quote from Marriner Eccles' *Beckoning Frontiers*, published in 1950, in which Eccles describes the forces that led to the Great Depression:

> As mass production has to be accompanied by mass consumption, mass consumption, in turn, implies a distribution of wealth—not of existing wealth, but of wealth as it is currently produced—to provide men with buying power equal to the amount of goods and services offered by the nation's economic machinery. Instead of achieving that kind of distribution, a giant suction pump had by 1929-30 drawn into a few hands an increasing portion of currently produced wealth. This served them as capital accumulations. But by taking purchasing power out of the hands of mass consumers, the savers denied to themselves the kind of effective demand for their products that would justify a reinvestment of their capital accumulations in new plants. In consequence, as in a poker game where the chips were concentrated in fewer and fewer hands, the other fellows could stay in the game only by borrowing. When their credit ran out, the game stopped.

(**Figure 8**)

Specifically, in the wake of the tax, regulatory, fiscal, saving, and financial policies that evolved over the thirty-five years leading up to the crash the mass markets necessary to support full employment were not achieved in the absence of an increase in debt relative to income as:

1.  Income was transferred to the top of the income distribution and the purchasing power out of income of the rest of the population relative to the output produced was reduced.

2.  Saving increased in the foreign sector by way of increasing trade deficits.

3.  Productivity increased even as domestic mass-production manufacturers were devastated by the undervalued exchange rates that led to the increases in international deficits.

4.  Full employment was achieved only through speculative bubbles.

Maintaining full employment through dissaving in the public sector and in a large portion of the private sector and increasing investment through speculative bubbles led to an increase in debt that was dramatically out of proportion to the growth in income. (**Figure 8**) This situation proved to be unsustainable in the long run as the system became unstable and eventually broke down in 2008 as debtors were una-

---

See also Reich's excellent documentary on this subject, Inequality For All (http://inequalityforall.com/watch-it-now/) and Blackford (2018, chs. 1-4 and 10-12).

ble to meet their financial obligations.[67]  It was the inability to continue to increase debt following the Crash of 2008 that led to the fall in the growth of consumption and to the diminished long-term expectation with regard to consumption that is the primal cause of the economic stagnation we experienced following the crash in 2008.

In other words, the economic stagnation that followed the Crash of 2008 arose from the fallout from Keynes' long-period problem of saving combined with what may be referred to as *the long-period problem of debt*, that is—*an inability to achieve and maintain the full employment of our resources in the absence of an increase in debt relative to income.*[68]

### IV-d. Income, Trade, and Technology

The basic competitive model that lies at the core of neoclassical economics implicitly assumes that wages and prices (including the prices of foreign currencies) *adjust automatically to redistribute income* in such a way as to maintain full employment as prospective yields and net saving/investment are forced

---

[67] See Acharya, Bair, Black, Bibow (Winter 2008/9; 2009), Blackford (2018, chs. 1-4, 7-8, 10-12), FCIC, Cohan, Cooper, Crotty (2009), Galbraith (2008, 2012), Gelinas, Johnson and Kwak, Krugman (2009), Levin and Coburn, Madrick, Mian and Sufi, Palley, Phillips (2008), Reich, Roubini, Stiglitz (2010), and Wessel, Atkinson et al, Atkinson and Morelli, Berg et al, Blanchard et al, Bordo and Meissner, Boushey et al, Iacoviello, Kumhof and Rancière, Kumhof et al,, Mian and Sufi, Morelli and Atkinson, Perugini et al, Rodrik (2014), Stiglitz, Zinman.

[68] See Atkinson et al, Atkinson and Morelli, Berg et al, Bibow (Winter 2008/9; 2009), Blackford (2018, chs. 1-4, 10-12), Blanchard et al, Bordo and Meissner, Boushey et al, Crotty (2009), Iacoviello, Kumhof and Rancière, Kumhof et al, Mian and Sufi, Morelli and Atkinson, Perugini et al, Rodrik (2014), Stiglitz, and Zinman .

to zero and economic profits are competed away.[69] There are no long-run adjustment problems that arise from an increase in the concentration of income, trade deficits, or the accumulation of capital or debt.

In the real world, however, prices do not adjust automatically to redistribute income so as to maintain full employment in the face of technological and institutional change. Economic profits are not competed away in the face of monopoly power, and economic rents are particularly inimical to the redistribution of income. There are long-run adjustment problems that arise from an increase in the concentration of income, trade deficits, and the accumulation of capital and debt, and the accumulation of capital in the midst of speculative bubbles can have dramatic effects on prospective yields when those bubbles burst and desired investment falls below desired saving.

Thus, there is no reason to believe the economy will be able to remain at full employment in the face of institutional and technological change that leads to trade deficits and an increase in the concentration of income as prospective yields, the rate of interest, and net saving/investment are forced to zero.[70] Nor is there a reason to believe that in the face of these changes the system will be able to maintain full employment in the absence of an increase in debt relative to income.

Since neoclassical models are typically presented in terms of a system of equations derived from the optimizing behavior of a representative household and

---

[69] See Krusell and Smith.

[70] Cf., Bibow (Winter 2008/9; 2009), Brynjolfsson and McAfee, Crotty (1990, 2002), Gordon, and Krusell and Smith.

firm the effects of institutional changes that lead to changes in the distribution of income are not explained in these models nor is the relationship between technology and the distribution of income. *Only the income of the representative household is explained* by way of the assumption that the amount of income the representative household receives is determined by the quantities of productive resources it owns and the prices these resources are able to command in the market *given the preferences of the representative household.* And only the technology embodied in the production function of the representative firm, *given the preferences of the representative household*, is considered in this model.

But the assumption that income is determined by the ownership of productive resources, in turn, implies that the distribution of income is ultimately determined by the distribution of wealth among households. This means that in order to examine how the distribution of income affects the economic system in a neoclassical model it is necessary to consider how the distribution of wealth/income can be expected to affect the *preferences of the representative household* and how these *preferences* and the *balance of trade* can be expected to affect the representative firm. When we do this we find that the distribution of wealth/income and the balance of trade have important implications with regard to the state of technology within the system.

If the representative household is to describe a closed economy with a high concentration of wealth/income it must be assumed that the preferences of the representative household that typifies this economy will favor outputs that serve the wealthy few rather than the bulk of the population through mass markets and that the representative firm will employ technologies that produce these kinds of outputs most efficiently. By the same token, if the representative household is to describe an open economy with a low concentration of wealth/income and a positive balance of trade it must be assumed that the preferences of the representative household that typifies this kind of society will favor those kinds of outputs that serve the bulk of the population through mass markets and that the representative firm will employ technologies that produce these kinds of outputs most efficiently.

Thus, even within the context of neoclassical economics, one is driven to the conclusion that—*in the absence of an unsustainable increase in debt relative to income*—within a closed economy the viability of mass-production technologies will be limited by the extent to which the concentration of income limits mass markets, and within an open economy the utilization of mass-production technologies will be limited by the country's balance of trade as well as the concentration of income. This means that these two factors set limits on productivity within the economic system: The higher the concentration of income and the lower the balance of trade, the fewer the opportunities to take advantage of mass-production technologies; the lower the concentration of income and higher the balance of trade, the greater the opportunities to take advantage of mass-production technologies.

As a result, Keynes' long-period problem of saving goes a long way toward explaining why developing countries with a high domestic propensity to save and concentration of income and a low balance of trade (low foreign-sector dissaving) have suffered from low productivity growth while those countries in a similar situation with a high balance of trade (high foreign-sector dissaving) that have adopted mass-production technologies while pursuing a policy of export-led growth were able to grow relatively rapidly leading up to the Crash of 2008.

At the same time, the long-period problem of debt goes a long way toward explaining why export-led growth has proved to be unsustainable in the long run as the *institutions* supporting employment in the importing countries led to a dramatic increase in debt relative to income. It is not surprising to find that the recent economic crisis began in the United States while it was running a substantial current account deficit in the midst of a massive speculative bubble as debt increased dramatically relative to income or that this crisis hit hardest in those countries that were in a similar situation.[71]

---

[71] See Bibow (Winter 2008/9; 2009), Blackford (2018, chs. 1-4, 7-12), Crotty (1990, 2002), FCIC, and Stiglitz (2014).

# Chapter V:
# Concluding Observations

*Those who cannot remember the past*
*are condemned to repeat it.*
George Santayana, 1905

Ignoring Keynes' analysis of the long-period problem of saving—combined with a failure to understand the way in which increasing debt relative to income is unsustainable in the long run—resulted in the adoption of economic policies that inhibited consumption and promoted saving and debt. These policies created a situation in which, given the state of mass-production technology, we could no longer achieve the full employment of our resources in the absence of an increase in debt relative to income. This is a road that inevitably leads to the kind of financial crisis that began in 2007 and to the economic stagnation that followed. It is also a road that can lead to the kinds of economic, political, and social problems we faced following the Crash of 1929, problems that eventually led to World War II.[72] It is, therefore, worth considering some of the differences as well as the similarities between these two crises.

## V-a. 1929, the Great Depression, and 2008
The series of events that led to the Great Depression began with a mild recession in the summer of

---

[72] See Acemoglu and Robinson, Boyer and Morais, Bernanke, Blackford (2018, chs. 3-4, 10-12), Domhoff (2014), Eichengreen, Friedman and Schwartz, Fisher (1932), Kennedy, Keynes (1933), Kindleberger, Lindert, Phillips, Piketty, Polanyi, Bullock, Shirer, Snyder, and Zinn.

1929 that became serious in the wake of the stock market crash that began in October of that year.

## *The Crash of 1929*

The Crash of 1929 began on October 24—a day that became known as Black Thursday—when the stock market dropped dramatically in the morning and recovered somewhat in the afternoon. While prices rallied on Friday, there were two more black days to come. When trading resumed following the weekend the Dow Jones Industrial Average fell by 13% on Black Monday and it fell an additional 12% the next day which became known as Black Tuesday. There were rallies that followed, but the crisis became severe following the Austrian *Credit-Anstalt* bank failure in May of 1930 followed by the failure of the Bank of the United States in December of that year. These two events led to a financial panic throughout Europe and the United States, a panic which led to the market loosing 80% of its value from 1929 to 1932 and the Dow falling by almost 90%—a panic that reached its climax in 1933 when over 4,000 commercial banks and savings institutions in the United States went under in that year alone.

In the meantime, consumer prices fell by 25% as output fell by over 30%, and 12.8 million people found themselves unemployed as the unemployment rate went from 3.2% of the labor force in 1929 to 24.9% in 1933. (**Figure 7**) By the time the crisis came to an end over 10,000 banks and savings institutions had failed along with a net loss of some 246,900 other businesses, and we were in the depths of the Great Depression—a worldwide depression that did not end until World War II was well underway. [73]

*Fallout from Depression and War*

The changes wrought by the Great Depression and World War II were truly astounding. In 1929 the international financial system was governed by the rules of the gold standard. France was a major colonial power. The sun never set on the British Empire. Britain was the most powerful nation on Earth and London the financial center of the world. America was an isolationist country with a mere ten percent of GDP devoted to government expenditures, virtually no military, and the labor movement had been almost beaten into submission. The Soviet Union, China, and Japan were third world countries, and the entire world, save the Soviet Union, was dominated by a free-market capitalist ideology. Then came the crash.

As the ensuing financial crisis and depression evolved the international financial system collapsed as Britain abandoned the gold standard in 1931, and the United States followed suit in 1933. Nations were crushed and governments fell around the world. The Nazis came to power in Germany and the Militarists in Japan. Japan invaded Manchuria in 1931. Italy invaded Ethiopia in 1935. The Spanish Civil War erupted in 1936, and Japan invaded China in 1937. Germany invaded Poland in 1939 then France in 1940 and the Soviet Union in 1941. When in July of 1940 the United States placed a gasoline and scrap iron embargo on Japan the fate of Pearl Harbor was sealed, and on December 7, 1941 the United States

---

[73] See Bernanke, Blackford (2018, ch. 4), Cohan, Eichengreen, Fisher (1932), Galbraith (1972), Kennedy, Keynes (1933), Kindleberger, Bullock, Shirer, Snyder, and Polanyi.

was drawn into the conflict.

When the dust settled from WW II 50 million people were dead, and the entire world had changed dramatically. Germany and Japan were devastated along with much of Russia, Britain, France, Italy, and most of Eastern Europe. The British Empire collapsed and France eventually lost her colonies as well. The League of Nations was replaced by the United Nations, which the United States decided to join after having shunned the League in 1920. The Bretton Woods Agreement established the International Monetary Fund and World Bank as the international Gold Standard was replaced by the dollar-exchange system. New York City became firmly entrenched as the financial capital of the world, and the United States became the world's most powerful nation and one of the most interventionist. All of Eastern Europe was dominated by the Soviet Union, and much of the world began to view communism as a viable alternative to capitalism as the Soviet Union went from being a third world country to becoming a super power.

Churchill gave his Iron Curtain speech at Westminster College in March of 1946, and in March of 1947 President Truman gave a speech before Congress that announced what came to be known as the Truman Doctrine. With that speech it became the official policy of the United States "to support free peoples who are resisting attempted subjugation" throughout the world, and the Cold War began in earnest. Within four years of war's end the Nationalists were driven out of Mainland China; China became a Communist country, and a new world order became entrenched.

### The Crash of 2008
The financial crisis that began in the summer of

2007 following the housing bubble bursting in 2006 had relatively little effect on the lives of ordinary people until the failure of Lehman Brothers in September of 2008. The rate of unemployment had increased gradually from its low of 4.4% in March of 2007 to 4.9% by April of 2008 as output continued to increase until the third quarter of 2007. The rate of unemployment accelerated a bit following Bear Stearns' failure in March of 2008 and had increased to 6.1% by August, but output had more or less stabilized. It was not until Lehman Brothers filed for bankruptcy in September followed by Congress's rejection of the Treasury's proposal to bail out the banks that a vicious downward spiral began in ernest.

The panic that followed resulted in a 48% fall in the S&P 500 stock index by the summer of 2009 and a 44% fall in the Dow. Output fell by 4% from the first quarter of 2008 through the second quarter of 2009 as the recession came to an end, and unemployment reached its peak at 10.0% in October of that year. Over 8 million people had lost their jobs by 2010 in the wake of the housing bubble bursting, and 4 million families lost their homes. In 2010, another 4.5 million families were seriously behind in their mortgage payments or were in the process of foreclosure. Nationwide, 10.8 million families—22.5% of all families with mortgages—owed more on their mortgages in 2010 than their houses were worth. In Florida, Michigan, and Nevada more than 50% of all mortgages were underwater.[74]

---

[74] Acharya and Richardson, Atkinson and Morelli, Bair, Baker, Black, Blackford (2018), Blanchard et al, Bordo, Cohan, Cooper, Crotty (2009), Cynamon and Fazzari, Dowd and Hutchinson, FCIC, Galbraith

## *How we Survived*

Even though the financial situation that led to the Crash of 2008 was much worse than that which led to the Crash of 1929, the fallout from the Crash of 2008 has, so far at least, been much less severe. There are three fundamental differences between then and now that have saved us from the kind of devastation wrought by the Crash of 1929: 1) the actions of the Federal Reserve, 2) the size of government relative to the economy, and 3) the existence of federal government social-insurance programs.

### Federal Reserve Actions

The actions taken by the Federal Reserve from 2007 through 2009 were truly heroic. By a) creating lending facilities that made available hundreds of billions of dollars to financial markets that were frozen, b) undertaking hundreds of billions of dollars of currency swaps with foreign central banks, and c) guaranteeing trillions of dollars worth of assets against default, the Federal Reserve (with the cooperation of the FDIC and Treasury) was able to prevent the disaster that would have occurred if financial institutions, either foreign or domestic, had been forced to dump trillions of dollars worth of asset-backed securities onto the market in a situation in which no one was willing to purchase those securities.

The actions of the Federal Reserve made unprecedented levels of reserves available to financial systems throughout the world as is indicated in **Figure 9**

---

(2008, 2012), Gelinas, Johnson and Kwak, Kumhof and Winant, Lansley, Levin and Coburn, Mian and Sufi, Palley, Phillips, Reich, Roubini and Mihm, Skidelsky (2012), Summers, Stiglitz (2010, 2012, 2014), Wessel, and Zinman.

by the dramatic increase in Federal Reserve Bank
Credit that occurred following the crash in 2008:

**Figure 9: Federal Reserve Bank Credit, 2003-2014.**

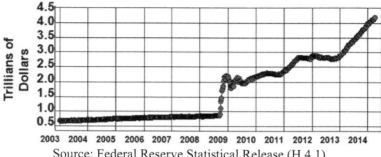

Source: Federal Reserve Statistical Release (H.4.1).

Without these reserves, our financial system most certainly would have collapsed in 2008, and the resulting
rate of unemployment would have been far above the
10% peak reached in 2009. In addition, because the
American dollar serves as a universally accepted reserve currency for international transactions, the collapse of our financial system would have brought
down the entire international financial system as well.

Through its actions, the Federal Reserve was able
to prevent a total collapse of both the domestic and
the international financial systems, and, as a result,
we have been able to avoid the consequences that resulted from the collapse of these systems in the 1930s:
a falling money supply combined with dramatically
falling wages and prices that led to the debt-deflation
cycle described by Irving Fisher in 1932.[75]

The situation was much different in 1929 through
1933. The Federal Reserve did increase its lending to
banks by 66% during this period, but it took four

---

[75] See also Bair, Blackford (2018), Crotty (2009), FCIC, and Wessel.

years to do so rather than four months as in 2008. To make matters worse, because of its free-market ideological faith in the self-correcting nature of markets, the Federal Reserve actually allowed Federal Reserve bank-credit to fall by 25% leading up to the banking crisis that began in 1930. To make matters even worse, there was no universally accepted international reserve currency in the 1930s that could be increased to deal with the international financial crisis that developed. There was only gold, and, as a result, the entire international financial system disintegrated as one country after another was forced to abandon that system.

It was the bold and decisive actions of the Federal Reserve that kept the domestic and world financial systems from disintegrating following the Crash of 2008 in the way it had disintegrated following the Crash of 1929.[76]

Size of Government

The importance of the second difference between then and now that has kept us from falling into the abyss we fell into in the 1930s—the size of government relative to the total economy—can be seen by noting that in spite of the fact that total government expenditures increased 14% from 1929 through 1933, total government expenditures were equivalent to only 10% of GDP in 1929 compared to 33% in 2008. Thus, the government's involvement in the economic system was much less in 1929 than it was in 2008, and the

---

[76] See Acharya and Richardson, Bair, Blackford (2018, chs. 3, 4, 10, and 11), Crotty (2009), Eichengreen (1995), FCIC, Friedman and Schwartz, Gailbraith (1972), Levin and Coburn, Meltzer, Kennedy, Kindleberger, Wessel.

government was not in as powerful a position to stabilize the system in 1929 as it was in 2008:

**Figure 10: Total Government Expenditures, 1929-2017.**

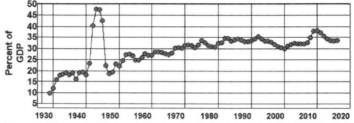

Source: Bureau of Economic Analysis, Table 1.1.5 and Table 3.1.

In addition, because of the ideological faith of policy makers in the self-correcting nature of markets government expenditures that contribute directly to GDP were actually allowed to fall by 14% as the depression began. This occurred because, even though the federal government's contribution to GDP remained fairly constant during this period and actually increased somewhat in 1933, this increase was more than offset by the fall in the state and local government expenditures that contributed to GDP. It was not until federal grants-in-aid to state and local governments began to increase in 1934 that the fall in the state and local government expenditures that contributed to GDP came to an end.[77]

During the recent crisis, the federal government's contribution to GDP increased by 24%, and due to a 41% increase in federal grants-in-aid to state and local governments their contribution to GDP increased by 7%.[78] The increases in total government expenditures and contribution to GDP during the current crisis

---

[77] See Blackford (2018, ch. 11).

[78] See Blackford (2014, ch. 11) and **Figure 11** below.

were the result of a) the size of the spending increases associated with automatic stabilizers such as unemployment compensation, food stamps, and other social-insurance programs[79] that automatically increase government spending in the face of an economic downturn, b) the Economic Stimulus Act passed on February 13, 2008, and c) the American Recovery and Reinvestment Act passed on February 17, 2009.

These actions helped to save us today because the resulting increases in government expenditures created income for people. This had the effect of short-circuiting the vicious downward spiral of falling employment, output, and income that wrought such havoc during the four years from 1929 through 1933 because the government-created income during the recent crisis partially offset the dramatic fall in incomes in the private sector of the economy. The stability of government expenditures in the face of the economic decline provided a powerful brake on the economy as it spiraled downward during the fall of 2008 through the summer of 2009 that was nowhere to be found in fall on 1929 through the summer of 1933.[80]

Social Insurance

The third difference between today and the 1930s that has kept us from falling into the abyss we fell into in the 1930s—one that has been essential to keeping us from suffering the kinds of deprivations and hardships that were so widespread in the 1930s—is the fact that a major portion of our federal government's budget is directly related to social-insurance pro-

---

[79] See Blackford (2014) for a breakdown of social-insurance expenditures in the federal budget.

[80] See Blackford (2018, chs. 10, and 11).

grams.[81] Not only did these programs provide a major contribution toward economic stability through the mechanism of automatic stabilization, there can be no doubt that the index of human misery and suffering that resulted from the economic, political, and social crisis that began in 2007 would have been immensely worse had it not been for the $2.3 trillion worth of government social-insurance expenditures that increased dramatically during the current crisis. Without these expenditures tens of millions of people would not have received these benefits, and we would have seen an increase in human suffering and misery as a result of the economic and human tragedy that began in 2008 far beyond that which actually occurred. In 2010 there were some 54 million beneficiaries in the Social Security system alone who would have had to face this tragedy without these benefits to fall back on if it had not been for the federal government.

There was no Social Security in 1929; no Medicare or Medicaid; no military or veterans' health benefits or pensions; no disability insurance or unemployment compensation; no food stamps, school lunch, or other food and nutrition programs; no housing assistance programs. When the crisis came people were left to fend for themselves as best they could, and the result was suffering and misery far beyond anything we see or can even imagine today. It was because of the immense personal hardship and suffering witnessed during the Great Depression that the federal government

---

[81] For a detailed breakdown of the federal budget and examination of the expenditures on each individual social-insurance program, see Blackford (2014).

was forced to step in, and the Federal Emergency Relief Administration (FERA), Public Works Administration (PWA), Civilian Conservation Corps (CCC), and Works Progress Administration (WPA) came into being in the 1930s.[82]  And it was because of the immense personal hardship and suffering witnessed during the Great Depression that the social-insurance programs saving us today—unemployment compensation, Social Security retirement and disability, veterans' benefits, Medicare, Medicaid, and school lunch/milk, food stamps, and other food and nutrition programs—came into being.

### *Where we Stand Today*

It is important to recognize, however, that even though we have been able to minimize the fallout from the Crash of 2008 and the recession that followed so far, none of the measures that have been taken to minimize this fallout have come to grips with the fundamental problem that brought us to where we are today.  Even though the fall in output and employment was reversed in the fourth quarter of 2009, and we have made some progress with regard to our trade deficits, these deficits seem to have stabilized at around 3% of GDP (**Figure 4**) and the concentration of income today is not only higher than in 2007, it is at a level comparable to that of 1928 and above where it was as the economy stagnated through the 1930s. (**Figure 6**) As a result, the economic recovery that began in 2009 has been far from satisfactory. [83]

---

[82]See Blackford (2018, chs. 5 and 10; 2014; chs. 3 and 4), Lindert, and Kennedy.

[83] According to the World Wealth & Income Database, the income share of the top 1% and 10% of the income distribution stood at 20%

## V-b. Keynes and the Great Depression

What is particularly disconcerting about the situation we face today is that in spite of the differences between the way in which we survived the recent financial crisis compared to the disaster that followed in the wake of the Crash of 1929 we do not seem to have learned the lessons that should have been learned from the Great Depression, World War II, and the economic prosperity that followed war.

As strange as it may seem, few economists seem to realize that, contrary to the conventional wisdom, the United States economy did not recover from the Great Depression.  What actually happened was the failure of the private sector to cope with the crisis that began in 1929 led to the New Deal and eventually to a government takeover of the economic system during World War II.  There were 8.1 million unemployed in the United States in 1940 after ten years of depression, and the unemployment rate did not fall below 14% until 1941. (**Figure 7**)  It was not until 1943 that this rate fell below the level in 1929.  By then we were fully mobilized for World War II, and employment in the military had increased by over 8.5 million men and women; non-federal debt as a fraction of GDP had fallen by 50% by 1945 from what it had been in 1940, and total debt as a percent of GDP was essentially held constant during and following the war. (**Figure 8**)

In other words, it was not until *after* the institu-

---

and 47% in 2014.  In 1928 the comparable numbers were 24% and 49%.  From 1930 through 1940 the top 1% and 10% averaged 17% and 45%, respectively, of total income. See also **Figure 12** – **Figure 14** below.

tional changes of the New Deal were in place, wage and price controls were instituted, the top marginal tax rate was increased to 94%, consumer goods were rationed, the production of consumer durables ceased, total government expenditures had risen to 48% of GDP, (**Figure 10**) non-federal debt was reduced dramatically relative to GDP, (**Figure 8**) and *the size of the military was increased by more than the number of unemployed in 1940* that the Great Depression finally came to an end.

This is what it took to end the Great Depression, and *it was the institutional changes* that occurred as a result of the New Deal and World War II—the rise of unions, adoption of a minimum wage, progressive taxation, government regulation of financial institutions, the capital controls of the Bretton Woods Agreement, and government investment in capital projects as well as in education, social-insurance, and innumerable other government programs—that led to the prosperity that followed the war, not an economic recovery as such.

As a result of these institutional changes, the economic system that emerged from the New Deal and World War II was not the system of *laissez-faire* that led us into the Great Depression:[84]

1.  The economic system that emerged from the New Deal and World War II was a system with a substantially reduced nonfederal debt relative to income (**Figure 8**) as a result of the rationing, wage and price controls, and the huge increase in government expenditures that had taken place during

---

[84] See Blackford (2018, chs. 4 and 6).

the war.

2. It was a system in which the capital control provisions of the Bretton Woods Agreement made it possible to keep our international balances in check (**Figure 4**) and in which financial regulatory institutions made it possible to achieve relatively full employment (**Figure 7**) in the absence of speculative bubbles.

3. It was a system in which the progressive tax structure put in place during the war (which remained largely intact for twenty years after the war) combined with the rise of unions, and an increasing minimum wage led to a reduction in the concentration of income as the income share of the bottom 90% of the income distribution increased from 54% of total income in 1933 to 69% by 1973 as the income share of the top 1% fell from 16% to 9% of total income. (**Figure 6**)

4. And it was a system in which a dramatic increase in the size of our domestic mass markets led to a dramatic increase in mass-production technology and productivity as the economic system in general thrived throughout the 1950s and 1960s in the absence of an increase in debt relative to income.[85]

Not only was the economic system that emerged from the New Deal and World War II not the system of *laissez-faire* that led us into the Great Depression, it was a system that embraced the *"somewhat com-*

---

[85] See Amy, Bernanke, Blackford (2018, chs. 1-4, 10-12), Boyer and Morais, Brynjolfsson and McAfee, Domhoff, Eichengreen, Fried man and Schwartz, Gordon, Kennedy, Kindleberger, Lindert, Meltzer, Perino, Piketty, Polanyi, and Zinn.

*prehensive socialisation of investment"* that Keynes had called for in the final chapter of *The General Theory* (p. 378) as the government made unprecedented *investments* in our defense and space programs; paved city streets, country roads, and built the U.S. and interstate highway systems; built and improved water and waste treatment facilities throughout the land along with ports and dams as it electrified vast regions of our country; expanded social-insurance, regulatory, educational, public health, and public safety systems as the role of government in the economic system expanded.

As a result of these *investments*, the capital stock grew and unemployment remained relatively low in defiance of Keynes' long-period problem of saving for some twenty-five years following World War II as the government's contribution to GDP increased from 9% of GDP in 1929 to 17% by 1950, and had reached 24% by 1970:

**Figure 11: Government Contribution to GDP
1929-2017.**

Source: Bureau of Economic Analysis, Table 1.1.5.

And throughout this period there was a negligible international balance, (**Figure 4**) and total debt relative to income decreased from 157% of GDP in 1945 to 141% in 1950, and had barely increased to 149% of

GDP by 1970 in defiance of the long-period problem of debt.[86] (**Figure 8**)

In other words, *it was the economics of Keynes' long-period problem of saving*, not the neoclassical economics of the Keynesians, that was validated by the New Deal, World War II, and the economic prosperity that followed the war. And the economics of Keynes was further validated by the institutional changes that occurred as a result of the policies adopted during and following the 1970s—suppression of unions, failure of the minimum wage to keep pace with inflation, regressive tax policies, financial deregulation, the abandonment of the capital controls of the Bretton Woods Agreement, failure to enforce antitrust laws, and government neglect of capital projects as well as education, social-insurance, and other government programs as government participation in the economic system diminished.

These are the policies that brought us to where we find ourselves today, faced with the fallout from Keynes' long-period problem of saving as the contribution of government to GDP fell from 24% in 1970 to

---

[86] It is also worth noting that according to Brynjolfsson and McAfee these three decades yeilded phenominal increases in productivity:

> In fact, when you look at history, you see that in the early years of the Great Depression, in the 1930s, productivity didn't just slow but actually fell for two years in a row—something it never did in the recent slump. Growth pessimists had even more company in the 1930s than they do today, but the following three decades proved to be the best ones of the twentieth century. Go back to figure 7.2 and look most closely at the dashed line charting the years following the dip in productivity in the early 1930s. You'll see the biggest wave of growth and bounty that the first machine age ever delivered. (p. 106)

Cf. Section **V-d** above.

19% in 2007 and by 2018 had fallen to 17% which is where it stood in 1950, far below the 23% average during the prosperous years of the 1950s and 1960s. (**Figure 11**)

At the same time, the concentration of income has risen to levels not seen since the 1920s (**Figure 6**) and trade deficits to levels not seen throughout the twentieth century (**Figure 4**), and we became overwhelmed by the long-period problem of debt as total debt increased from 149% of GDP in 1970 to 349% by 2007 leading up to the Crash of 2008 and was still at 333% of GDP in 2018. (**Figure 8**)

It should not have been a surprise that in the wake of the institutional changes that began in the 1970s total debt rose to the unsustainable levels that led to the Crash of 2008 as the concentration of income increased to levels comparable to those leading up to the Crash of 1929. Nor should it have been a surprise that the system failed to recover to its prerecession trends (**Figure 12**) in the face of persistent trade deficits and the increased concentration of income in the absence of speculative bubbles and the failure of debt to increase relative to income. Or that the labor force participation rate (**Figure 13**) has fallen dramatically as well. These are the kinds of results that should have been expected from the attempt to reverse the institutional changes and "somewhat comprehensive socialisation of investment" that led us out of the Great Depression and into the prosperity that followed World War II. Why should any of this have been a surprise? After all, what we are talking about here is an attempt to reestablish *laissez-faire*, a system plagued by the same long-period problem of saving and debt that not only led to the Crash of 2008

### Figure 12: Trends in Real GDP, 1950-2017.

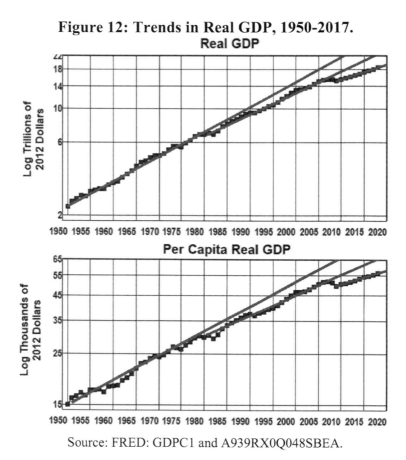

Source: FRED: GDPC1 and A939RX0Q048SBEA.

### Figure 13: Labor Force Participation Rate, 1950-2017.

Source: Bureau of Labor Statistics, Labor Force Statistics.

and the economic stagnation that followed, but to the Crash of 1929 and the Great Depression as well—*a world-wide depression* that led to World War II.[87]

## V-c. Lessons not Learned

It may seem counterintuitive in today's world, deluged as we are with so much antigovernment rhetoric, but the simple fact is, *it was the government, not the private sector*, that ended the Great Depression and led to the prosperity that followed World War II, and *it was the government, not the private sector*, that kept us from falling into the abyss we fell into in the 1930s in the aftermath of the Crash of 2008.

This is the lesson that should have been learned from the Great Depression and the prosperity that followed World War II and from the recent crisis as well. But instead of learning this lesson we see the powers that be in the developed countries of the world attempting to further cut the size of the government that led us out of the Great Depression into the prosperity that followed the war and to roll back the social insurance programs that have saved us so far from the kinds of deprivations and misery that led to the social and political chaos we experienced during the 1930s that led to World War II.

To make matters worse, there has been very little progress in dealing with the fundamental causes of the economic stagnation we face today. As was noted above, the trade deficits in the United States seem to

---

[87] See Blackford (2018, chs. 1-4, 6-8, and 10-12), Bullock, Eichengreen, Kennedy, Keynes (1933), Kindleberger, Piketty, Shirer, Snyder, Polanyi, and Marriner Eccles quoted in footnote 69 above.

have stabilized at around 3% of GDP, and the concentration of income today is at a level comparable to that of 1928 and significantly above where it was as the economy stagnated through the 1930s. And, not surprisingly, we also see the beginnings of the same kinds of political and social unrest we saw in the 1930s, not only in the United States, but throughout much of the rest of the world as well. This does not bode well for the future.[88]

**V-d. Looking to the Future**

There are, of course, a number of factors that have the potential to offset the effects of Keynes' long-period problem of saving—specifically, to offset the tendency for the MEC to fall as saving increases the capital stock over time—factors such as population growth, technological change that increases the demand for capital and consumption goods, and an increasing balance of trade. It may even be possible to offset this tendency through economic policies that foster the kinds of speculative bubbles and increases in debt relative to income that made it possible for employment to increase and unemployment to fall in spite of the accompanying increase in trade deficits and the concentration of income that we witnessed for twenty-five years leading up to the Crash of 2008.

But there are limits to these offsets, and in light of the economic history of the nineteenth through the beginning of the twenty-first century it would take either an extraordinary degree of ideological blindness or a giant leap of blind faith for anyone who knows anything about this history to believe these offsets can be relied upon by way of *laissez-faire* to avoid the

---

[88] See Snyder, Bullock, and Shirer.

kinds of economic, political, and social catastrophes that were experienced during this period of history.[89]

The history of the nineteenth through the beginning of the twenty-first century clearly shows that the institutional changes that resulted from the New Deal and World War II are *essential* in combating the effects of the long-period problem of saving and its companion the long-period problem of debt. This is obvious from the way in which the expanded role of government in the economic system led to the economic prosperity that followed the war, not only in the United States, but in those countries in North America and Western Europe that adopted similar changes compared to the lack of prosperity in those that did not.[90] This is also obvious from the way in which the systematic dismantling of these institutions beginning in the 1970s led to the Crash of 2008 and the economic stagnation that followed.[91]

---

[89] See Acemoglu and Robinson, Acharya, Akerlof, Alperovitz and Daly, Amy, Baker, Beckert, Brynjolfsson and McAfee, Bernanke, Black, Blackford (2018), Boyer and Morais, Bruner, Carson, Cohan, Cooper, Cowie, Crotty, Cynamon and Fazzari, Deaton, Domhoff, Dew-Becker and Gordon, Eichengreen, Farmer, FCIC, FDIC, Fisher (1932), Friedman and Schwartz, Galbraith, Garcia et al., Gelinas, Gordon, Graeber, Hansen (1939), Harrington, Hartmann, Hansen (1939), Harvey, Henriques, Hobson, Johnson (2006), Johnson and Kwak, Josephson, Kennedy, Kindleberger, Keynes (1933; 1936), Klein (2007), Krugman, Kuttner, Lakoff, Lansley, Lewis, Lindert, Lowenstein, MacKay, Mian and Sufi, Meltzer, Minsky, Morris, Palley, Perino, Phillips, Piketty, Polanyi, Reich, Reinhart and Rogoff, Rodrik, Roubini and Mihm, Sachs, Schumpeter, Bullock, Shirer, Snyder, Skidelsky, Stewart, Stiglitz, Taleb, Veblen, Wessel, and Zinn.

[90] See Acemoglu and Robinson, Amy, Blackford (2019, ch. 1), Dowd and Hutchinson, Henriques, Klein (2007), Kuttner, Lindert, Musgrave, Rodrik (2011), and Smith.

[91] See Blackford (2018).

To effect institutional change by way of the imperatives of depression and war is hardly an optimal way to achieve economic growth and prosperity. It makes much more sense to address this problem proactively than to wait for the inevitable economic, political, and social catastrophe that results from economic stagnation and collapse and hope for the best. But avoiding catastrophe requires that the problem be understood and confronted directly.

There can be little hope for the future so long as economists are unable to come to a clear understanding of Keynes' long-period problem of saving in a way that leads to an overwhelming consensus within the discipline of economics to the effect that—*consumption is the driving force for economic growth and employment, not saving.*

The failure of economists, both Keynesians and anti-Keynesians alike, to face this reality and address it directly is a serious mistake. Only by facing this reality and addressing it directly will it be possible to affect the *institutional changes* needed to solve Keynes' long-period problem of saving proactively, hopefully, in a way that will make it possible to avoid yet another worldwide conflagration that, in this nuclear age, is likely to be even more devastating than the one that began on September 18, 1931 and reached its climax on August 6, 1945.

# Bibliography

Acemoglu, Daron and James Robinson. (2012) *Why Nations Fail: The Origins of Power, Prosperity and Poverty*. New York: Crown.

Acharya, Viral and Matthew Richardson (Editors), (2009) *Restoring Financial Stability: How to Repair a Failed System*. John Wiley & Sons.

Ackley, Gardner. (1957) Liquidity Preference and Loanable Funds Theories of Interest: Comment. *American Economic Review,* 47, 662-73.

―――, (1961) *Macroeconomic Theory*. New York: Macmillan.

Akerlof, George and Robert J. Shiller. (2009) *Animal Spirits: How Human Psychology Drives the Economy, and Why It Matters for Global Capitalism*. Princeton: Princeton University Press.

Alperovitz, Gar and Lew Daly. (2008) *Unjust Deserts: How the Rich Are Taking Our Common Inheritance*. New York: New Press.

Amy, Douglas J. (2011) *Government is Good: An Unapologetic Defense of a Vital Institution*. Indianapolis: Dog Ear Publishing.

Asimakopulos, A. (1983) Kalecki and Keynes on Finance, Investment and Saving, *Cambridge Journal of Economics*. 7, 221–233.

―――. (1986) Finance, liquidity, saving and investment, *Journal of Post Keynesian Economics*. 9. 79-90.

Atkinson, Anthony B. and Salvatore Morelli. (2010) *Inequality and Banking Crises: A First Look*. Report for the International Labour Organization.

―――. (2011) Economic Crises and Inequality," UN Development Program Human Development Research Paper 2011.06.

————. (2015) Inequality and crises revisited. Economia Politica: Journal of Analytical and Institutional Economics, 31-51.

Atkinson, Tony, Joe Hasell, Salvatore Morelli, Max Roser. (2017) Chartbook of Economic Inequality. INET Oxford Working Paper.

Bair, Sheila. (2012) Bull by the Horns: Fighting to Save Main Street from Wall Street and Wall Street from Itself. New York: Free Press.

Baker, Dean. (2009) *Plunder and Blunder: the Rise and Fall of the Bubble Economy*. Sausalito, CA: Poli-Point Press.

Barro, Robert J. and Hershel I. Grossman (1971) A General Disequilibrium Model of Income and Employment. *American Economic Review*, pp. 82-93.

Beckert, Sven (2015) *Empire of Cotton: A Global History*. Vintage Books.

Berg, Andrew, Jonathan Ostry, and Jeromin Zettelmeyer. (2012) What Makes Growth Sustained? *Journal of Development Economics.* 149-166.

Bernanke, Ben S. (2000) *Essays on the Great Depression*. Princeton: Princeton University Press.

————. (2005) The Global Saving Glut and the U.S. Current Account Deficit. Updates speech given on March 10, 2005, at the Sandridge Lecture, Virginia Association of Economists, Richmond, Virginia, April 14, 2005. https://www.federalreserve.gov/boarddocs/speeches/2005/20050414/default.htm.

Bibow, Jörg. (1995) Some reflections on Keynes's 'finance motive' for the demand for money *Cambridge Journal of Economics.* 19, 647-666, reprinted with amendments in Bibow (2009).

————. (2000a) The Loanable Funds Fallacy in Retrospective, *History of Political Economy.* 32:4, 769-831, reprinted with amendments and a postscript in Bibow

(2009).

————. (2000b) On exogenous money and bank behavior: the Pandora's box kept shut in Keynes' theory of liquidity preference? *The European Journal of the History of Economic Thought.* 7:4, 532-568, reprinted with amendments in Bibow (2009).

————. (2001) The loanable funds fallacy: exercises in the analysis of disequilibrium. *Cambridge Journal of Economics.* 25 (5), 591-616, reprinted with amendments in Bibow (2009).

————. (2005) Liquidity Preference Theory Revisited—To Ditch or to Build on It? Working paper 427, The Levy Economics Institute of Bard College. Reprinted with amendments in (2007) Arestis, Philip and Malcolm Sawyer Ed *A Handbook of Alternative Monetary Economics.* Edward Elgar Publishing.

————. (Winter, 2008/9) Insuring against Private Capital Flows: Is It Worth the Premium? What Are the Alternatives? *International Journal of Political Economy.* 37:4,

————. (2009) Keynes on Monetary Policy, Finance and Uncertainty: Liquidity Preference Theory and the Global Financial Crisis. Routledge.

Black, William K. (2013) The Best Way to Rob a Bank Is to Own One: How Corporate Executives and Politicians Looted the S&L Industry. Austin: University of Texas Press.

Blackford, George H. (1975) Money and Walras' Law in The General Theory of Market Disequilibrium. *Eastern Economic Journal*, 1-9.

————. (1976) Money, Interest, and Prices in Market Disequilibrium: A Comment. *Journal of Political Economy*, 893-894.

————. (2014) *Understanding the Federal Budget.* Amazon.com: www.rwEconomics.com.

————. (2018) *Where Did All The Money Go? How Lower Taxes, Less Government, and Deregulation Redistribute Income and Create Economic Instability.* 2nd edition, Amazon.com: www.rwEconomics.com.

————. (2019) *Essays on Political Economy: Volume II: Keynes.* Amazon, www.rwEconomics.com.

————. (2020) *Essays on Political Economy: Keynes: Volume III: Keynes.* Amazon, www.rwEconomics.com.

Blanchard, Olivier J., David Romer, A. Michael Spence, and Joseph E. Stiglitz (editors). (2012) *In the Wake of the Crisis. Leading Economists Reassess. Economic Policy.* Cambridge, Mass: MIT Press.

Bordo, Michael and Christopher Meissner. (2012) Does Inequality Lead to a Financial Crisis? *Journal of International Money and Finance,* 2147–61.

Borio, Claudio and Piti Disyatat. (2011) Global imbalances and the financial crisis: Link or no link? Bank of International Settlements Working Paper, No 346.

Boushey, Heather, J. Bradford DeLong, Marshall Steinbaum. (2017) *After Piketty: The Agenda for Economics and Inequality*, Harvard University Press.

Boyer, Richard O. and Herbert M. Morais. (1979) *Labor's Untold Story: The Adventure Story of the Battles, Betrayals and Victories of American Working Men and Women.* United Electrical, Radio & Machine Workers of America.

Brady, Michael Emmett. (1994) Keynes, Pigou and the Supply Side of the General Theory. *History of Economics Review, pp.* 34-46.

————. (1995) A Study of J. M. Keynes' Marshallian-Pigouvian Elasticity Approach in Chapter 20 and 21 of the GT. *History of Economics Review. 55-*71.

Brothwell, John F. (1986) 'The General Theory' after Fifty Years: Why Are We Not All Keynesians Now? *Journal of Post Keynesian Economics.* 8:4, 531-547.

Bruner, Robert F. (2007) *The Panic of 1907: Lessons Learned from the Market's Perfect Storm.* Hoboken: John Wiley & Sons.

Brunner, Karl. (1950) Stock and Flow Analysis: Discussion. *Econometrica,* 246-51.

Brynjolfsson, Erik and Andrew McAfee. (2014) *The Second Machine Age: Work, Progress, and Prosperity in a Time of Brilliant Technologies.* W. W. Norton & Company.

————. (2015) Will Humans Go the Way of Horses? *Foreign Affairs.* https://www.foreignaffairs.com/articles/2015-06-16/will-humans-go-way-horses

Bullock, Alan. (1952) Hitler: *A Study in Tyranny.* New York: Harper.

Carson, Rachel. (1962) *Silent Spring.* London: Penguin Books.

Clower, Robert W. (1965) The Keynesian Counter-Revolution: A Theoretical Appraisal. In F. Hahn and F. Breeching, eds., *The Theory of Interest Rates.* New York: St. Martin's Press.

————. (1975) Reflections on the Keynesian Perplex. *Zeitschrift für Nationalökonomie / Journal of Economics.* 1-24.

Cohan, William D. (2009) House of Cards: A Tale of Hubris and Wretched Excess on Wall Street. New York: Anchor Books.

Cohen, Avi J. and G. C. Harcourt (2003) Whatever Happened to the Cambridge Capital Theory Controversies? *Journal of Economic Perspectives.* 199-214.

Cooper, George. (2008) The Origin of Financial Crises: Central Banks, Credit Bubbles and the Efficient Market Fallacy. Petersfield, Great Britain: Harriman House.

Cowie, Jefferson R. (2010) *Stayin' Alive: The 1970s and the Last Days of the Working Class.* New York: New

Press.

Crotty, James R. (1980) Post-Keynesian Economic Theory: An Overview and Evaluation. *The American Economic Review, Papers and Proceedings*, *70*, 20-25.

———. (1990) Keynes on the Stages of Development of the Capitalist Economy: The Institutional Foundation of Keynes's Methodology. *Journal of Economic Issues*, 24, 761-780.

———. (2002) Why There Is Chronic Excess Capacity. *Challenge*, 45, 21-44.

———. (2009) Structural Causes of the Global Financial Crisis: A Critical Assessment of the 'New Financial Architecture'. *Cambridge Journal of Economics*. 563-580.

Cynamon, Barry Z. and Steven M. Fazzari. (2014) Inequality, the Great Recession, and Slow Recovery. SSRN.

Davidson, Paul. (1965) Keynes' Finance Motive. *Oxford Economic Papers*, 47-65.

———. (1967) The importance of the demand for finance, *Oxford Economic Papers*, 19, 245–253.

———. (1972) A Keynesian View of Friedman's Theoretical Framework for Monetary Analysis. *Journal of Political Economy*, 80, 864-82.

———. (1978) *Money and the Real World*, 2nd edition, London, Macmillan.

———. (1986) Finance, funding, saving, and investment, *Journal of Post Keynesian Economics*, 9, 101-110.

De Scitovszky, Tibor. (1940) A Study of Interest and Capital. *Economica,* 7 (27), new series, 293-317.

Deaton, Angus. (2013) *The Great Escape: Health, Wealth, and the Origins of Inequality*. Princeton University Press.

Dew-Becker, Ian and Robert J. Gordon. (2005) Where Did The Productivity Growth Go? Inflation Dynamics And

The Distribution Of Income, Brookings Papers on Economic Activity, v2005 (2), 67-150.

Domhoff, G. William. (1967) *Who Rules America?* Prentice Hall.

———. (1986) Who Rules America Now? A View From the 80s. Prentice-Hall, Inc.

———. (2012) The Myth of Liberal Ascendancy: Corporate Dominance from the Great Depression to the Great Recession. Paradigm.

Dowd, Kevin and Martin Hutchinson. (2010) Alchemists of Loss: How modern finance and government intervention crashed the financial system. John Wiley & Sons.

Dunlop, John T. (1938) The Movement of Real and Money Wage Rates. *The Economic Journal*, vol. 48, no. 191, pp. 413–434.

Eccles, Marriner S. (1950) *Beckoning Frontiers: Public and Personal Recollections*, ed. Sidney Hyman (New York: Alfred A. Knopf.

Eichengreen, Barry. (1995) *Golden Fetters: The Gold Standard and the Great Depression, 1919-1939*. Oxford: Oxford University Press.

———. (2015) Hall of Mirrors: The Great Depression, the Great Recession, and the Uses—and Misuses—of History. Oxford: Oxford University Press.

Farmer, Roger E. A. (2010) *Expectations, Employment, and Prices*. New York: Oxford University Press.

FCIC. (2011) The Financial Crisis Inquiry Report, Authorized Edition: Final Report of the National Commission on the Causes of the Financial and Economic Crisis in the United States. New York: Public Affairs.

FDIC. (1997) *History of the Eighties: Lessons for the Future*. Washington, DC: Federal Deposit Insurance Corporation.

Fellner, W. and Somers, H. M. (1941) Alternative Monetary Approaches to Interest Theory. *Review of Eco-*

*nomics and Statistics*, 23, 43-8.

Fisher, Irving. 1930. The Theory of Interest: As Determined by Impatience to Spend Income and Opportunity to Invest It. New York: Macmillan.

———. (1932) *Booms and Depressions*. Adelphi Co.

Fleisher, B. M. and K. J. Kopecky. (1987) The Loanable-Funds Approach to Teaching Principles of Macroeconomics. *The Journal of Economic Education*, 19-33.

Freeman, Joshua B. (2000) *Working-Class New York: Life and Labor Since World War II*. New York: New Press: Distributed by W.W. Norton.

Friedman, Milton. (1949) The Marshallian Demand Curve. *Journal of Political Economy*, LVI, 463-95.

———. (1957) *A Theory of the Consumption Function*. Princeton: Princeton University Press.

Friedman, Milton and Anna J. Schwartz. (1963) *A Monetary History of the United States, 1867-1960*. Princeton University Press.

Galbraith, James K. (2008) The Predator State: How Conservatives Abandoned the Free Market and Why Liberals Should Too. New York: Free Press.

———. (2012) Inequality and Instability: A Study of the World Economy Just Before the Great Crisis. Oxford University Press.

Galbraith, John K. (1958) *The Affluent Society*. Houghton Mifflin.

———. (1966) *The New Industrial State*. Houghton Mifflin.

———. (1972) *The Great Crash, 1929*. Boston: Houghton Mifflin.

Garcia, Gillian, Carl-Johan Lindgren, and Matthew I. Saal. (1996) *Bank Soundness and Macroeconomic Policy*. Washington, D.C.: International Monetary Fund.

Gelinas, Nicole. (2011) *After the Fall: Saving Capitalism from Wall Street and Washington*. New York: Encounter Books.

Giraud, Yann. (2014) Negotiating the "Middle-of-the-Road" Position: Paul Samuelson, MIT, and the Politics of Textbook Writing, 1945–55. *History of Political Economy* 46 (annual suppl.), 134-52.

Gordon, Robert J. (2016) The Rise and Fall of Economic Growth: The U.S. Standard of Living Since the Civil War. Princeton University Press.

Graeber, David. (2011) *Debt: The First 5,000 Years*. Melville House.

Grossman, Hershel I. (1971) Money, Interest, and Prices in Market Disequilibrium. *Journal of Political Economy.* pp. 943-61.

Haberler, Gottfried. (1941) *Prosperity and Depression*. Geneva: League of Nations.

Hansen, Alvin. H. (1939) Economic Progress and Declining Population Growth. *The American Economic Review*, 1-15.

————. (1953) *A Guide to Keynes*. New York: McGraw Hill.

Harrington, Michael. (1962) *The Other America: Poverty in the United States*. New York: McGraw-Hill.

Hartmann, Thom. (2007) *Screwed: The Undeclared War Against the Middle Class - And What We Can Do about It*. San Francisco: Berrett-Koehler Publishers, Inc.

Harvey, David. (2005) *A Brief History of Neoliberalism*. Oxford: Oxford Univ. Press.

Hawtrey, R. G. (1933) Mr. Robertson on 'Saving and Hoarding'. *Economic Journal*, 43, 701-08.

Hayek, Friedrich. (Aug. 1931) Reflections on the Pure Theory of Money of Mr. J. M. Keynes, Part I. *Economica,* 270-951.

————. (Nov. 1931) A Rejoinder to Mr. Keynes. *Economica*, 398-403.

————. (1932) Reflections on the Pure Theory of Money of Mr. J. M. Keynes, Part II. *Economica*, 12, 22-44.

Hayes, M. G. (2006) *The Economics of Keynes: A New Guide to The General Theory*, London: Edward Elgar.

Henriques, Diana B. (2000) The White Sharks of Wall Street: Thomas Mellon Evans and the Original Corporate Raiders (Lisa Drew Books) Scribner.

Hicks, John R. (1936) Keynes' Theory of Employment. *Economic Journal*, 238-53.

————. (1937) Mr. Keynes and the 'Classics'; A Suggested Interpretation. *Econometrica*, 147-59.

————. (1946) Value and Capital: An Inquiry into Some Fundamental Principles of Economic Theory, Second Edition. Oxford University Press.

Hobson, John A. (1965) *Imperialism: A Study*. University of Michigan Press.

Horwich, George. (1964) *Money Capital and Prices*. Homewood: Irwin.

Hume, David. 1739. *A Treatise of Human Nature.* International Relations and Security Network, Eth Zurich, Last accessed 2/9/2018:

https://people.rit.edu/wlrgsh/HumeTreatise.pdf

Huntington, James B. (2011) *Work's New Age: The End of Full Employment and What It Means to You*. Royal Flush Press.

Hume, David. 1739. *A Treatise of Human Nature.* International Relations and Security Network, Eth Zurich, Last accessed 2/9/2018:

https://people.rit.edu/wlrgsh/HumeTreatise.pdf

Iacoviello, Matteo. (2008) Household Debt and Income Inequality, 1963–2003. *Journal of Money, Credit and Banking*, 929– 965.

Jaffe, William. (1967) Walras' Theory of Tâtonnement: A Critique of Recent Interpretations. *Journal of Political*

*Economy*, 1-19.

Johnson, Harry. (1952) Some Cambridge Controversies in Monetary Theory. *Review of Economic Studies*, 90-104.

──────. (1961) The General Theory After Twenty-Five Years. *American Economic Review*, 1-17.

──────. (1962) Monetary Theory and Policy. *American Economic Review*, 335-77.

Johnson, Haynes. (2006) *The Age of Anxiety: McCarthyism to Terrorism*. Mariner Books.

Johnson, Simon and James Kwak. (2010) *13 Bankers: The Wall Street Takeover and the Next Financial Meltdown*. New York: Vintage Books.

──────. (2012) White House Burning: The Founding Fathers, Our National Debt, and Why it Matters to You. New York: Vintage Books.

Josephson, Matthew. (1934) *The Robber Barons: the Great American Capitalists, 1861-1901*. New Brunswick: Transaction Publishers.

Kennedy, David M. (1999) *Freedom from Fear: The American People in Depression and War*. 1929-1945. Oxford University Press.

Keynes, John M. (1924) *A Tract on Monetary Reform*. Macmillan: London.

──────. (1930) *A Treatise on Money*. Ed. Austin Robinson and Donald Moggridge (2013), *The Collected Writings of John Maynard Keynes*, Vol. V, Cambridge University Press.

──────. (Sept. 1931) Mr. Keynes' Theory of Money: A Rejoinder. *Economic Journal*, 412-23.

──────. (Nov. 1931) The Pure Theory of Money: A Reply to Dr. Hayek. *Economica*, 387-97.

──────. (1933) National Self-Sufficiency, *The Yale Review*, 22:4, 755-769.

──────. (1936) *The General Theory of Employment, Inter-*

*est, and Money*. New York: Harcourt, Brace and Co.

———. (Sept. 1936) Fluctuations in Net Investment in the United States. *Economica*, 540-47.

———. (Feb. 1937) The General Theory of Employment. *Quarterly Journal of Economics*, 209-23.

———. (June 1937) Alternate Theories of the Rate of Interest. *Economic Journal*, 241-52.

———. (Dec. 1937) The '*ex-ante*' Theory of the Rate of Interest. *Economic Journal*, 663-69.

———. (1938) Mr. Keynes and 'Finance'. *The Economic Journal*. 314-322.

———. (Sep. 1939) The Process of Capital Formation. *Economic Journal*, XLIX, 569-74.

———. (Feb. 1939) *The General Theory of Employment, Interest and Money*. Preface to the French Edition, at Project Gutenberg Australia. Retrieved, 2011:
http://gutenberg.net.au/ebooks03/0300071h/frapref.html

———. (1946) The Theory of the Rate of Interest. *Lessons of Monetary Experience Essays in Honor of Irving Fisher*, reprinted in *Readings in the Theory of Income Distribution*, ed. W. Fellner and B. F. Haley, Philadelphia, 418-24.

———. (1978) Some Economic Consequences of a Declining Population. *Population and Development Review*, Vol. 4, No. 3, 517-523.

———. (1979) The Collected Writings of John Maynard Keynes, the General Theory and After: A Supplement. XXIX, ed., D. Moggridge, Macmillan.

Kindleberger, Charles P. (1986) *The World in Depression, 1929-1939: Revised and Enlarged Edition*. University of California Press.

Klein, Lawrence R. (1966) *The Keynesian Revolution*. New York: Macmillan.

———. (1950) Stocks and Flow Analysis in Economics. *Econometrica*, 236-46.

Klein, Naomi. (2007) *The Shock Doctrine: The Rise of Disaster Capitalism.* Toronto: Alfred A. Knopf.

Kohn, Meir. (1981) A Loanable Funds Theory of Unemployment and Monetary Disequilibrium. *American Economic Review*, 859-79.

Kregel, J. A. (1976) Economic Methodology in the Face of Uncertainty: The Modeling Methods of Keynes and the Post-Keynesians. *The Economic Journal*, 86: 342, 209-225.

Krugman, Paul. (2004) *The Great Unraveling: Losing Our Way in the New Century.* New York: W.W. Norton.

————. (2009a) The Return of Depression Economics and the Crisis of 2008. New York: W.W. Norton.

————. (2009b) *"How Did Economists Get It So Wrong?"* New York Times:

https://www.nytimes.com/2009/09/06/magazine/06Economic-t.html

Krusell, Per and Anthony A. Smith Jr. (2015) Is Piketty's "Second Law of Capitalism" Fundamental? *Journal of Political Economy*, 725-748.

Kuhn, Thomas S. (1970) *The Structure of Scientific Revolutions.* University of Chicago Press.

Kumhof, Michael and Romain Rancière. (2010) Inequality, Leverage and Crises. IMF Working Paper.

Kumhof, Michael, Romain Rancière, and Pablo Winant. (2015) Inequality, Leverage, and Crises. *American Economic Review*, 1217– 1245.

Kuttner, Robert. (1999) *Everything for Sale: The Virtues and Limits of Markets.* University of Chicago Press.

————. (2008) The Squandering of America: How the Failure of Our Politics Undermines Our Prosperity. New York: Vintage Books.

Kuznets, Simon (1953) *Shares of Upper Income Groups in Income and Savings.* Cambridge, MA: National Bureau of Economic Research.

————. (1955) Economic Growth and Income Inequality. *American Economic Review* 45, no. 1, 1–28.

Kwak, James. (2017) *Economist: Bad Economics and the Rise of Inequality.* Pantheon Books: New York.

Lakoff, George. (2008) The Political Mind: Why You Can't Understand 21st-Century American Politics with an 18th-Century Brain. New York: Viking.

Lansley, Stewart. (2012) *The Cost of Inequality: Why Economic Equality is Essential for Recovery.* London: Gibson Square.

Lavoie, Marc and Wynne Godley. (2007) *Monetary Economics: An Integrated Approach to Credit, Money, Income, Production and Wealth.* New York: Palgrave Macmillan.

Leijonhufvud, Axel. (1968) *On Keynesian Economics and the Economics of Keynes.* Oxford University Press.

————. (2006) "Keynes as a Marshallian" in Backhouse, R. and B. Bateman, Eds. *The Cambridge Companion to Keynes.* Cambridge University Press, pp. 58-77.

Lerner, Abba P. (1938) Alternative Formulations of the Theory of Interest. *Economic Journal*, 211-30.

————. (1944) Interest Theory - Supply and Demand for Loans or Supply and Demand for Cash. *Review of Economic Statistics*, 88-91.

Levin, Carl and Tom Coburn. (2011) *Wall Street and the Financial Crisis: Anatomy of a Financial Collapse.* D.C.: Permanent Subcommittee on Investigations.

Lewis, Michael. (1989) *Liar's Poker: Rising Through the Wreckage on Wall Street.* New York: W.W. Norton & Company.

Lindert, Peter H. (2004/5) *Growing Public: Social Spending and Economic Growth Since the Eighteenth Century,* Volume 1 and Volume 2. Cambridge: Cambridge University Press.

Lloyd, Clifford. (1964) Lord Preference and Lord Funds.

*The Economic Journal*, 578-581.

Lowenstein, Roger, (2002) *When Genius Failed: The Rise and Fall of Long-Term Capital Management*. London: Fourth Estate.

MacKay, Charles. (1841) *Extraordinary Popular Delusions and the Madness of Crowds*. New York: Harmony, 1980.

Madrick, Jeff. (2014) Seven Bad Ideas: How Mainstream Economists Have Damaged America and the World. New York: Alfred A. Knopf.

Marshall, Alfred. (1920) *Industry and Trade*, 3rd edition, New York: The Macmillan Company.

————. (1961) *Principles of Economics*, 9th edition. New York: Macmillan.

Meltzer, Allen H. (2003) *A History of the Federal Reserve*. Volume 1: 1913-1951, Chicago, University of Chicago Press.

Mian, Atif and Amir Sufi. (2014) House of Debt: How They (and You) Caused the Great Recession, and How We Can Prevent It From Happening Again. Chicago: University of Chicago Press.

Minsky, Hyman P. (1986) *Stabilizing an Unstable Economy*. New Haven: Yale University Press.

————. (1992) The Financial Instability Hypothesis: An Interpretation of Keynes and an Alternative to 'Standard' Theory. *Nebraska Journal of Economics and Business*, 5-16.

Modigliani, Franco. (1944) Liquidity Preference and the Theory of Interest and Money. *Econometrica*, XII, 45-88.

Morelli, Salvatore and Anthony B. Atkinson. (2015) Inequality and Crises Revisited. *Economia Politica*, 1 31-51.

Morris, Charles R. (1999) *Money, Greed, and Risk: Why Financial Crises and Crashes Happen*. New York:

Times Business.

Musgrave, Richard. (1959) *The theory of public finance; A study in public economy*. New York: McGraw-Hill.

Ohlin, Bertil G. (March 1937) Some Notes on the Stockholm Theory of Savings and Investment, Part I, *Economic Journal*, 47, 53-69; 47, 221-40.

———. (June 1937) Some Notes on the Stockholm Theory of Savings and Investment, Part II. *Economic Journal*, 221-40.

———. (Sept. 1937) Alternate Theories of the Rate of Interest: Three Rejoinders. *Economic Journal*, 423-27.

Palley, Thomas I. (2012) *The Economic Crisis: Notes From the Underground*. Washington, DC: Thomas I. Palley.

Patinkin, Don. (1958) Liquidity Preference and Loanable Funds: Stock and Flow Analysis. *Economica*, 25, 301-18.

———. (1959) Reply to R. W. Clower and H. Rose. *Economica*, 253-5.

———. (1965) Money, Interest and Prices: An Integration of Monetary and Value Theory. New York: Harper & Row.

———. (1976) Keynes and Econometrics: On the Interaction the Macroeconomic Revolutions of the Interwar Period." *Econometrica,* 1091-1123.

Perino, Michael. (2010) The Hellhound of Wall Street: How Ferdinand Pecora's Investigation of the Great Crash Forever Changed American Finance. New York: Penguin Press.

Perugini, Cristiano, Jens Holscher, and Simon Collie. (2013) Inequality, Credit Expansion and Financial Crises. Munich Personal RePEc Archive, 51336.

Phillips, Kevin P. (2008) Bad Money: Reckless Finance, Failed Politics, and the Global Crisis of American Capitalism. New York: Viking.

———. (2002) Wealth and Democracy: A Political History

of the American Rich. New York: Broadway Books.

Piketty, Thomas. (2014) *Capital in the Twenty-first Century,* trans. A. Goldhammer. Harvard Univ. Press.

———. (March 2014) *Technical appendix of the book « Capital in the twenty-first century.* Harvard University Press: http://piketty.pse.ens.fr/files/capital21c/en/Piketty2014 TechnicalAppendix.pdf.

Polanyi, Karl. (1944) The Great Transformation: The Political and Economic Origins of Our Time. Farrar & Rinehart.

Reich, Robert. (2010) *Aftershock: The Next Economy and America's Future.* New York: Vintage Books.

Reinhart, Carmon M. and Kenneth S. Rogoff. (2009) *This Time Is Different: Eight Centuries of Financial Folly.* Princeton, New Jersey: Princeton University Press.

Robertson, Dennis H. (1931) Mr. Keynes' Theory of Money. *Economic Journal*, 395-411.

———. (Sept. 1933) Saving and Hoarding. *Economic Journal*, 399-413.

———. (Dec. 1933) Mr. Robertson on 'Saving and Hoarding. *Economic Journal*, 109-12.

———. (Nov. 1936) Some Notes on Mr. Keynes' General Theory of Employment. *Quarterly Journal of Economics*, 168-91.

———. (June 1937) Alternate Theories of the Rate of Interest: Three Rejoinders. *Economic Journal*, 428-36.

———. (June, 1938) Mr. Keynes and 'Finance'. *Economic Journal*, 314-22.

———. (Sept., 1938) Mr. Keynes and 'Finance'. *Economic Journal,* 555-6.

———. (1940) *Essays in Monetary Theory.* P. S. King: London.

———. (1959) Lectures on Economic Principles III. Staples: London.

Robertson, Dennis H. and J.M.K. (June, 1938) Mr. Keynes and "Finance". *The Economic Journal*. 314-322.

Robinson, Joan. (1951) The Rate of Interest. *Econometrica*, 92-111.

Rodrik, Dani. (1997) *Has Globalization Gone Too Far?* D. C. Institute for International Economics.

————. (2011) The Globalization Paradox: Democracy and the Future of the World Economy. New York: W.W. Norton & Co.

————. (2014) Good and Bad Inequality. Project Syndicate.

————. (2017) Economics Rules: The Rights and Wrongs of the Dismal Science. W. W. Norton & Company.

Rose, Hugh. (1957) Liquidity Preference and Loanable Funds. *Review of Economic Studies*, 111-19.

————. (1959) The Rate of Interest and Walras' Law. *Economica,* 252-3.

Roubini, Nouriel and Stephen Mihm. (2010) *Crisis Economics: A Crash Course in the Future of America*. Penguin Press.

Sachs, Jeffrey D. (2008) *Common Wealth: Economics for a Crowded Planet*. Penguin Press.

Schlefer, Jonathan. (2012) *The Assumptions Economists Make*. Cambridge: Harvard University Press.

Schumpeter, Joseph A. (1942) *Capitalism, Socialism, and Democracy*. Boston: Unwin.

Shackle, George L. S. (1961) Recent Theories Concerning the Nature and Role of Interest. *Economic Journal,* 209-54.

Shirer, William L. (1960) *The Rise and Fall of the Third Reich; A History of Nazi Germany*. New York: Simon and Schuster.

Skidelsky, Robert. (2003) *John Maynard Keynes 1883-1946: Economist, Philosopher, Statesman*. New York: Penguin Books.

————. (2012) *Keynes: The Return of the Master*. London: Penguin Books.

Smith, Yves. (2010) ECONned: How Unenlightened Self Interest Undermined Democracy and Corrupted Capitalism. St. Martin's Press.

Snyder, Timothy. (2017) *On tyranny twenty lessons from the twentieth century*. New York: Tim Duggan Books.

————. (2019) *The Road to Unfreedom*. Random House.

Stewart, James B. (1992) *Den of Thieves*. New York: Simon & Schuster.

Stiglitz, Joseph E. (1999) Interest Rates, Risk, and Imperfect Markets: Puzzles and Policies. Oxford Review of Economic Policy, Vol.15, No.2, *Real Interest Rates,* Oxford University Press*,* 59-76.

————. (2010) Freefall: America, Free Markets, and the Sinking of the World Economy. New York: W. W. Norton & Company, Inc.

————. (2012a) Macroeconomic Fluctuations, Inequality, and Human Development. Columbia University Academic Commons,

————. (2012b) The Price of Inequality: How Today's Divided Society Endangers Our Future. New York: W. W. Norton & Company, Inc.

————. (2014) Reconstructing Macroeconomic Theory to Manage Economic Policy. NBER Working Paper No. 20517.

————. (2015) The Great Divide: Unequal Societies and What We can do About Them. New York: W. W. Norton & Company, Inc.

Summers, Lawrence. (2014) U. S. Economic Prospects: Secular Stagnation, Hysteresis, and the Zero Lower Bound. *Business Economics*, 49, 65-72.

Taleb, Nassim. (2007) *The Black Swan: The Impact of the Highly Improbable*. Random House.

Tarshis, Lorie. (1939) Changes in Real and Money Wages.

*The Economic Journal*, vol. 49, no. 193, pp. 150–154.

Teigen, Ronald L. (1964) Demand and Supply Functions for Money in the United States: Some Structural Estimates. *Econometrica,* 476-509.

Terzi, A. (I986a) Finance, saving and investment: a comment on Asimakopulos. *Cambridge Journal of Economics*, 10:1.

———. (I986b) The independence of finance from saving: a flow-of-funds interpretation, *Journal of Post Keynesian Economics*.

Tsiang, Sho-Chieh. (1956) Liquidity Preference and Loanable Funds Theories, Multiplier and Velocity Analysis: A Synthesis. *American Economic Review*, 539-64.

———. (1957) Liquidity Preference and Loanable Funds Theories of Interest: Reply. *American Economic Review*, 673-78.

———. (1966) Walras' Law, Say's Law and Liquidity Preference in General Equilibrium Analysis. *International Economic Review*, 329-45.

———. (1980) Keynes' 'Finance' Demand for Liquidity, Robertson's Loanable Funds Theory, and Friedman's Monetarism. *Quarterly Journal of Economics*, 467-90.

Veblen, Thorstein. (1900) *The Theory of the Leisure Class*. Macmillan.

———. (1904) The Theory of Business Enterprise. Transaction Books.

Walras, Leon. (1954) *Elements of Pure Economics*, trans by Jaffe. London: George Allen and Un-win.

Weintraub, E. Roy. (2002) Neoclassical Economics. *The Concise Encyclopedia of Economics*. Liberty Fund, Inc.

Wessel, David. (2009) *In Fed We Trust: Ben Bernanke's War on the Great Panic*. New York: Three Rivers Press.

Wray, L. Randall. (1990) *Money and credit in capitalist*

*economies: the endogenous money approach.* Edward Elgar Publishing Company.

————. (Winter, 2003-2004) Loanable Funds, Liquidity Preference, and Endogenous Money: Do Credit Cards Make a Difference? *Journal of Post Keynesian Economics*, 309-323.

Zinman, Jonathan. (2015) Household Debt: Facts, Puzzles, Theories, and Policies. *Annual Review of Economics*, 251– 276.

Zinn, Howard. (2003) *A People's History of the United States: 1492-Present.* New York: Harper Collins.

Zouache, Abdallah. (2004) Towards a 'New Neoclassical Synthesis'? An Analysis of the Methodological Convergence between New Keynesian Economics and Real Business Cycle Theory. *History of Economic Ideas*, 95-110.

# Name Index

Gordon..89, 95, 120, 138, 145, 152, 155
Graeber......109, 145, 155
Grossman.....99, 148, 155
H. Johnson .............. xi, 97
Haberler............... xi, 155
Hahn .........................151
Hansen 73, 74, 94, 96, 98, 145, 155
Harcourt.............151, 158
Harrington .........145, 155
Hartmann...106, 145, 155
Harvey...............145, 155
Hasell .........................148
Hawtrey ...20, 27, 28, 155
Hayek . 7, 10, 11, 155, 157
Hayes ...............5, 95, 156
Henriques ....94, 145, 156
Hicks... ix, 1, 2, 26, 35, 67, 94, 96, 97, 156
Hobson..........iii, 145, 156
Holscher.....................162
Horwich..... xi, 34, 73, 156
Hume .........................156
Huntington.................156
Hutchinson116, 117, 128, 145, 153
Iacoviello...108, 116, 117, 119, 156
Jaffe .............41, 156, 166
Johnson...x, xi, 60, 61, 94, 97, 108, 109, 116, 117,

119, 129, 145, 157
Josephson .........145, 157
Kalecki.......................147
Kennedy....124, 126, 131, 135, 138, 143, 145, 157
Keynes... i, ii, v, vi-xvi, 1-6, 8- 33, 35-42, 45-49, 51-55, 5-60, 62, 63, 65, 67-70, 72-75, 77, 79-81, 83-85, 87-98, 100, 102-104, 111-114, 119, 122, 124, 126, 136, 139, 140, 143-150, 152, 155-166
Kindleberger .....109, 116, 117, 119, 124, 126, 131, 138, 143, 145, 158
Klein ... xi, 2, 4, 68, 69, 74, 94, 104, 108, 109, 111, 145, 158, 159
Kohn............... xi, 34, 159
Kopecky........... xi, 96, 154
Kregel........................159
Krugman ...108, 119, 145, 159
Krusell ...............120, 159
Kuhn....................10, 159
Kumhof .....108, 116, 117, 119, 129, 159
Kuttner.47, 106, 145, 159

Printed by Amazon Italia Logistica S.r.l.
Torrazza Piemonte (TO), Italy

11326727R00114